Cleaning Up in Your Service Business

Brian W. Appleton

OASIS PRESS BOOKS & SOFTWARE

The Oasis Press® / PSI Research
Central Point, Oregon

This publication is designed to provide accurate and authoritative information in regard to the subject matter covered. It is sold with the understanding that the author and publisher are not engaged in rendering legal, accounting, or other professional service. If legal advice or other expert assistance is required, the services of a competent professional person should be sought.
— from a declaration of principles jointly adopted by a committee of the American Bar Association and a committee of publishers.

Edited by Carolyn Appleton
Interior design by Eliot House Productions
Cover illustration and design by J. C. Young

Please direct any comments, questions, or suggestions regarding this book to
The Oasis Press®/PSI Research:

    Editorial Department
    P.O. Box 3727
    Central Point, Oregon 97502
    (541) 245-6502
    (541) 245-6505 fax
    info@psi-research.com *e-mail*

The Oasis Press® is a Registered Trademark of Publishing Services, Inc., an Oregon corporation doing business as PSI Research.

Appleton, Brian W., 1939-
    Cleaning up in your service business / by Brian W. Appleton ; edited by Carolyn Appleton.
      p. cm.
    ISBN 1-55571-537-0 (pbk.)
      1. Service industries—United States. 2. New business enterprises—United States. 3. Entrepreneurship—United States. I. Appleton, Carolyn. II. Title.

HD9981.5 .A67 2000
658.1'141—dc21   00-047827

Printed in the United States of America
First Edition 10 9 8 7 6 5 4 3 2 1

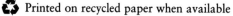 Printed on recycled paper when available

Contents

Section II

To my best friend and beautiful wife, Carolyn. She has with her intelligence, writing, and secretarial skills managed to make any project I undertake look good for nearly four decades.

Introduction

The basic secret to succeeding in almost any business today seems elusive to many entrepreneurs, but it really is no mystery. My father once said to me, "When it comes to starting a successful business, find a need and fill it."

What is missing when you look at many businesses these days? Service. No matter what type of business it is, provide genuine service and you will always have customers.

When you last called for a repairman or an estimate on a home improvement job, were you impressed by the service — or were you depressed by the lack of service? When you were at a store checkout and they took ten minutes to check on a price for an item clearly marked on sale, only to have a clerk claim the tag was put on the wrong item, how did you feel? How about the last time you were sick — so sick you could hardly sit up — and how long did you have to wait to see the doctor?

There is a golden opportunity for people who go into business today. Why? Because there is a desperate need in most areas of business for real service. If you go into your new business with the attitude that you are at their service, rather than the other way around, you multiply your chance of success.

There are many areas wherein a business can succeed or fail. Most will tell you it is under-financing, bad location, etc. Yet consider this: these may only be factors. After more than 30 years of helping others start businesses, I am absolutely convinced that in most cases the success or failure of a small business is due to its owner's attitude. When you come face to face with a customer, the correct attitude is, "I am at your service." Believe it and succeed. A service business that I started years ago with $450 produced a gross profit of $160,000 a year in a short time; and I operated it *part-time*. That correct attitude had to be maintained in my case, as it will in yours. You must never forget that you are at the customer's service, not the other way around.

In these pages you will find guidelines to help the average person who needs a higher income in today's escalating economy. Perhaps you are a capable but downsized executive who needs to match your previous level of income with an inexpensive entry-level business. It is also a guide for students working their way through school so as not to put a heavy burden on their parents. Finally, it will serve as a tutor to the person who wants to keep his or her present job but needs a profitable additional income.

Why talk mainly about the service business? Why not some of the other more glamorous types of businesses found out there? Simply put, it is a matter of *money*. You can make more and invest less than most businesses available. Perhaps that is why service businesses are among the fastest growing in our economy. Perhaps that is why nearly half of the top low-investment business franchises in the United States are service businesses.

I realize that pricing can vary greatly in different parts of the country. (For example: Marble floor refinishing might pay as much as $25 per square foot in New York, or as little as $2 per square foot in Miami.) But you've got to start somewhere. Therefore, this book will give you an overall average for that particular business, as well as an idea of the basis on which the pricing is structured. You will need to adjust it realistically after you get started.

Besides the low start-up costs for service businesses, within a few years of successful operation a healthy six-figure income is possible — and I have seen many do it!

Suddenly, within the last decade, the equipment used in many of these businesses has gone high tech. Thus you can expect to do a better job with less time and effort by using the new technology.

Service businesses are also good because you can control how big you want to become. For example, the international cleaning company, I.S.S., boasts over 50,000 employees. However, you can make a very good living and have time to enjoy life if you maintain a modest-sized operation. This can be true even if you choose to do it all yourself. A young grocery store clerk started a parking lot cleaning service and expanded his one-man operation from a $1,500 investment to a $120,000 a year business — still working it alone.

You will notice that the majority of the service businesses covered are some sort of cleaning service. There are a number of good reasons for this. First, it is the part of the service business industry I personally have worked in for most of my career. Thus the examples are for some sort of cleaning service. Secondly, the cleaning services are very profitable, easy to get into with a minimum investment and education — although completion of at least high school is recommended. They are always in demand and can be adapted to almost any industrial or domestic locations. However, there are many other types of service businesses available. If you look, almost daily you will see a new situation where an entrepreneur could provide a service and fill a need in the community.

I have operated a diversified service business for over 25 years, employing just over 50 people. By some standards this is still small. However, I have found that this size business can operate even in a small town and I can go home at night without the stress a larger business could bring. As a result, I have been able to take advantage and do some of the things that are more important to me, such as enjoying my family and some very rewarding volunteer work. I have also worked as a consultant in the successful start-up of over 125 other service businesses and taught small business at a local college.

This book is divided into two parts. Section 1 will cover the basics of how to start and maintain a service business. The principles you will learn apply to the many service businesses listed and discussed in Section 2. As you get into Section 2, you will see how the various businesses interrelate and where you can easily increase profits by adding on an additional service. Many people don't diversify because they do not know how to price the new services. *What sets this book apart from others is its specific pricing information, with hard-to-find pricing information given for each specialty, as well as an Appendix providing names, addresses, internet addresses, and phone numbers for suppliers and sources of additional training for your chosen field.*

Treat this book as a textbook. Don't just read this book, study it. One student took my course on business that covers the principles in the first part of this book. Upon completion, she said she had learned more in two months than she had previously learned in four years of college preparing for her MBA. That's good, because that's my goal — to epitomize and simplify; to help a student learn what is absolutely necessary as quickly as possible. Take advantage of the subtle details that will guide you not just in starting your business, but will make you a leader in your market area. Pitfalls and how to avoid them are also discussed. May you find success and profit in your chosen endeavor, but most of all, may you enjoy what you are doing.

— Brian W. Appleton

Section I

An Idea Is Born

"If you are possessed by an idea, you find it expressed everywhere, you even smell it."

—Thomas Mann (1903)

If you are like most people, you have been working at a full-time job requiring 40 or more hours a week. Or perhaps you are still in school, anticipating a long career working for a large corporation, hoping the boss will recognize your abilities and give you a chance for advancement. For the majority of us, even those with leadership ability, the chance just doesn't come.

Why not make it come by starting your own business? But what kind of business should it be? How much money would you have to invest? Also, how will you live until you get your venture off the ground?

These are valid considerations that deserves further exploration.

The Idea

To begin with, you must have an idea of what you would like to do. Assess your interests and abilities. Maybe you love plants and thought a landscaping service, spending each day with your hands in the soil, would be more like recreation than work. Or perhaps you enjoy the satisfaction of making things that are soiled look new again. Then some aspect of cleaning — a maid service or a janitorial office cleaning service — may sound good to you.

You should not dismiss certain ideas right away. Sometimes successful entrepreneurs have found themselves running a business they first thought they would not like. When the idea of running a contract office cleaning service was suggested to me, my first thought was, "I don't like to clean!" But you know, I actually got to enjoy taking something dirty and making it look good. Then, as the business grew, I enjoyed the challenge of overseeing large facilities and putting some ideas I had to work on a large scale.

- Education
- Experience
- Interests
- Abilities

How do you know what areas to pursue? Assess your (1) education, (2) experience, (3) interests, and (4) abilities.

Education

Are you a college student or graduate? What courses have you taken? Don't limit yourself to the courses for your degree, but think of other courses you took. For example, did you take an accounting course as an alternate to your major in English literature? That accounting course may be your ticket to the successful management of a service business. Or, with a little more training, it could even be your service business. There are people who drive from one small business to another each month bringing their clients books up to date and make a very good living at it.

Don't dismiss any possibility. Think back to your high school days. Were you always looking forward to shop class? Maybe you have a talent for working with your hands. Maybe working as an independent contractor in some aspect of the construction industry will have you looking forward to going to work every day.

Thinking of what will sell as well as what you were taught may give you some ideas for your new business undertaking. Your idea must be practical for your market (i.e., there's no future selling snow blowers in Florida), but don't limit yourself to what everyone else is doing.

Experience

Job experience is an important consideration. Obviously you would look at what you have done in the past. However, if you look beyond any job experience you may have, you may discover an area many overlook. What about experience you have that is not related to a paying job?

Many people are involved with clubs, church, or civic organizations. Maybe you were asked to oversee a function. Or a friend may have asked you to help put together a large wedding. This involved gathering equipment and people to do a job, organizing the work, and getting everything done just right and on time. This called for people skills, job skills, and organizational ability. Maybe you had to do all this within a budget. Sounds a lot like running a small business, doesn't it?

So, once again, put on that thinking cap and list all the things you have done already that may help you as you start your own service business.

Interests

Of course, you want to be happy in your chosen field. So honestly assess where your interests lie.

A word of caution: As you recall, I said I did not like to clean and found myself in the cleaning business for 25 years. I did like the money and the freedom the business afforded me. You may change your mind, so keep your mind open to new ideas.

Make a list of things you like to do — hobbies, sports, etc. These may give you an idea. Many have turned their hobby into their business. Do you, for example, find yourself at your computer every free minute you have? Perhaps a service using this interest will suit you. Besides the obvious areas, such as computer programming or Web page design, there are other ways knowledge of computers can pay off. In Section 2, one potential idea for a service business is Computer and Office Machine Cleaning. Some have also expanded this service to computer clean room cleaning.

Are you athletic, can't wait for the weekend to get to enjoy the outdoors? Maybe you can enjoy the outdoors all week with a pressure washing service or window cleaning service.

Abilities

Now is the time for a reality check. If you are a total klutz, maybe working with your hands is not for you. If you have organizational skills, put them to work for you. This is often where the maximum level of income is. Hire others to do the things you can't do well, and watch your income soar.

If you can't do something, don't give up. Enlist the help of someone who can. Watch and maybe you can do it yourself next time. Several people in business today learned just that way.

Money

Think of all the people who have had a good idea but did not know how to get the money to implement their plan. (Maybe automobiles would have been invented a few hundred years ago.) The appeal of most service businesses is that most can be started with a minimum investment.

By and large, you will not have to invest in inventory, and if you start out small, you and maybe some of your family will be the staff. Equipment will be your greatest initial expense. A future chapter will discuss how even this expense can be minimized by a technique that has worked well for many.

If you must obtain a loan to get started, shop carefully. You can easily get a loan from a finance company — however, most charge anywhere from 20 to 35 percent interest. Your credit card, too, can be expensive. So start with the best bets. Banks and savings and loan institutions usually offer the best interest rates. Look professional when you go in to see the manager of your bank. Go prepared with figures and information as to the potential income from your business venture — in other words, a business plan.

The business plan will reveal to the banker whether you know what you are doing. A good plan can be as many as 25 pages, but I recommend one as succinct as possible. Often a few well-organized pages are enough. It should show the banker that you've done your research and you understand where your business will be financially a few years down the road. It should also provide convincing evidence that you can return their money with minimum risk. Since this document is so important, I recommend you get some qualified help from a professional when putting it together. Perhaps the least expensive way would be to read the book *Before You Go into Business Read This* by Ira N. Nottonson, published by Oasis Press. It will help you write your plan yourself, and that is often the best way to do it.

Also, be aware that many banks promote a home equity line of credit, based on the equity in your home. If you don't own a home, other items of value can be used as collateral. Prepare a list of all your assets before going into the bank. If you are turned down, go to another bank, and another, until you have either gotten your loan or seen every bank in town. Only then will you want to pursue financing by a higher-interest source.

When purchasing equipment, if you already have the work to justify the expense, you also can ask your bank for a 90-day note. Bankers will often give a 90-day note quicker than a long-term loan. The benefit to you will be interest savings and no long-term obligation. You may even see if the distributor of the equipment has a leasing program.

Credit unions are also a very good source of financing at a reasonable interest rate. If one is available to you, you may wish to look into this possibility.

Finally, you may need to pursue what you thought about first: speaking to a friend or relative about making or co-signing a loan. This should be the last resort, not the first. If you want to maintain your relationship with your friend or relative, put all the terms in writing, sign it, and do everything in your power to pay on time. "It's only money," you may say, but it can easily destroy a relationship. So think carefully before pursuing this source of revenue.

How to Get Started without Starving

Service businesses have the unique potential of being something you can start on a part-time basis, while you keep your current job. Perhaps your family can pull together, with one keeping his or her job while the other begins to build up the service business. But careful planning is essential.

It is important to come up with a working plan that grows as you can afford it, rather than borrowing a large amount of money to invest in equipment, frills, or other things that can wait. Some businesses open with a fancy office, a fleet of trucks, and a large staff. They look impressive but are often gone a year later. I started working out of my home part time. My wife helped out with the typing and bookkeeping. And we all, including our daughter, went out on the job when needed. Other than word-of-mouth, our only marketing was a Yellow Pages listing. Our business grew at a steady pace. When we were ready, we built a small office with high visibility and again kept our budget in proportion to our income, thus avoiding large debt that eats up profits.

Keep careful books and know where your money is going and how much is profit. Poor money management can destroy your business. A later chapter will show a simplified method for keeping your books.

Picking a Name

This is almost an afterthought for many, but it is very important. Perhaps due to ego or lack of imagination, most businesses end up with the owner's name: Joe's Cleaning Service or Smith's Lawn Service. This may work for you, but the image is of a man in dirty coveralls driving an old pickup truck.

How you name your business has much to do with the market you want. You will also want to be sure to allow for the future. Five years down the road you may see an opportunity to diversify into a lucrative new area. You may start out with a window cleaning service and later branch out into pressure washing, or painting. The name Joe's Window Service will confine you. Also, if you sell your business after a number of years, a business name without your personal name in it is more marketable.

Think of image. Seek to dignify your business. Look through your phone book listings. What strikes you as a name that will cause those fingers to stop walking and start dialing? Some find using the name of the city, area, or a geographical feature engenders local support for your business. If your line is security, a strong name, one that will convey peace of mind to the customer, is appropriate. In these increasingly frightening times, people want to feel they have made a safe choice. So present yourself as someone who is reliable in whatever business you pursue. Also, if you pick a name that begins with a letter high in the alphabet, it gets top billing in the phone book (i.e., AAA Service, Inc.).

A name can also give the image of a large, successful company that has a staff of well-qualified personnel on hand. Even if you start out working out of your home, your family can help a lot if they all learn basic business telephone etiquette.

When you have decided on a name, the next thing will be to decide on whether to incorporate. One advantage of incorporation is that you will have a measure of protection for your personal assets, such as your home, against lawsuits. However, you are then an employee of this new entity you have created, and there may be certain taxes involved that would not be required of a sole proprietor or partnership. In most cases, although your tax structure may differ, you will end up paying about the same in taxes.

There also are a couple different kinds of corporations available. Here the advice of a good lawyer or tax expert is well worth the cost. Also, don't overlook the possibility of forming a limited liability company (LLC). The LLC is not a partnership nor is it a corporation. It is relatively new and combines the advantages of a corporation with a partnership. An advantage of the LLC is its tax flexibility. While you are visiting that lawyer, also draw up the paperwork needed to file the name you have chosen as your legal name, thus protecting your business name from being used by others. If you are a sole proprietor, you will automatically gain the name of doing business as, or d/b/a. Thus you will be "Joe Smith, d/b/a Valley Service Associates."

In Conclusion

As mentioned in the Introduction, if you want to succeed in business, find a need and fill it. Be observant. What service businesses do you see in your area? Do you see something that people would pay for that is not being done?

For example, some enterprising people have started a service delivering restaurant food. A private company will take your order for any of a number of restaurants, pick up your food, and deliver it to your home or hotel room, for a fee. Sharp idea! If you haven't heard of it, your area could be wide open for just such a service business.

If you think carefully, you can probably find a number of things you can do. Be open to the possibilities. Follow through and you will succeed.

Marketing Your Business

*The best mental effort in the game of business is concentrated
on the major problem of securing the consumer's
dollar before the other fellow gets it.*

—Stuart Chase

Start-up manuals abound for most types of business. But most of them fail to
tell you *how* to get the business. What good is knowing how to run a business
if you don't have any customers?

Like it or not, you will have to get out and *sell* your service. Most people put
trying to sell something right next to having a root canal as a favorite thing to
do. But if you are going to succeed in this business, you are going to have to
learn to overcome this mental block — and it is indeed more than anything else
a mental block. You must make regular public relations (PR) calls on established customers and sales calls on new ones. In other words, you must learn
how to market your product — that is, your service. Accept it.

There is the option of buying a franchise and letting them help you with the
sales work and organization. Prepare to pay an initial franchise fee of $2,500
to $15,000 and more. Add to that 5 to 20 percent of your yearly gross for their
help. If you absolutely feel you don't want to face people and ask them for their
business and you have that much start-up money, then that may be the way for
you to go. However, most franchises will ultimately expect you to do your own

sales work after their initial efforts. If you want to look into that approach further, there is a listing of some of the top franchises in the Appendix of this book.

Assuming, however, you want to take a more economical approach, there are some things you can do that will make it easier for you.

First Impressions

As you prepare for this part of your work, the key to success is to give careful thought to your dress, business cards, letterheads, and overall appearance.

Make your first impression by creating a good overall appearance.

If your chosen business provides a service to the business community, you will be calling on business people. Show respect for them by dressing like a businessperson. Look sharp. Be well groomed, well dressed, and carry neat sales materials. If you will be providing a service to homeowners, the principle is the same. You must instill confidence and trust. A clean, sharp appearance is essential.

Sales Materials

Your business card is the cheapest and most effective piece of advertising you will every buy. Forget Joe's Bargain Cards at $9.95 per thousand. Spend a little more and get the best looking cards you can find. They will pay off. The same principle goes for your letterhead and other printed matter. In addition to these printed items, many service businesses use a sales manual. It is a valuable tool that will help you (even if you are shy) to sell your service. You can put together a sales manual by following these simple steps:

1. Purchase a one-inch, clear-overlay, three-ring binder.

2. Take your new card and slide it under the overlay ... or, better yet, use a computer printing program to design and print an attractive cover with your company name on it. (Perhaps a "quick printer" copy service can help you with this.)

3. Inside, include the following:

   - A page of your references, including your bank.

   - A list of any customers you already have who can be contacted to check on your service.

- Pictures of locations.

- Pictures of yourself as well as your workers in their uniforms on the job. (I will address uniforms later.)

- A copy of a blank proposal form.

- A copy of a typical written agreement. (Some prefer not refer to it as a contract — it frightens some smaller accounts.)

- Any other visual aids that will impress a prospective client.

Of course, in time you will improve the contents of your sales manual, but never underestimate its value. You are not selling a product you can place on the desk in front of your prospect. You are selling an invisible service, a promise to perform. The visual aids in your sales manual are very important. Try to show it to every prospect.

Lastly, just before you get to the sensitive subject — money — you might add a touch of humor. Tastefully done, this takes the edge off. A couple of ideas that have worked; "You know why our people are so diligent, Mr. Smith? It's because of our head supervisor, Harry." Turning the page, there is a large picture of a silverback lowland gorilla. Or you might say, "Our people are so good because (turning the page to reveal a picture of your children busy at work around the house) we train them from infancy." I usually use this approach just before asking for a chance to quote a price.

All set! Check the mirror — looking sharp. Check the sales materials — all ready.

Show Time

> *The world is governed by appearance rather than by realities, so that it is fully as necessary to seem to know something as to know it.*
>
> —Daniel Webster

OK, you have your sharp-looking business cards in your pocket, your new sales manual in your hand, and you are ready to go. What do you do now?

There are a number of ways to effectively contact customers. There is no one perfect way. Try them all and decide which one works for you and your area.

Cold Call

This basically means starting on one side of town and working every prospect that might use your service until you call on all of them. Don't be put off if you are turned down on your first visit. For this work, you must keep notes as to who you contacted, what degree of interest was expressed, and then call back ... and call back ... and call back — as many times as it takes to get the business.

For residential work, a polite telephone call or flyer will produce some prospects. Target the neighborhoods you think most promising. Keep good records of names and dates you called. If they indicated they might be interested in the future, be sure to get back to them. As with calls on businesses, the sale is most often made on follow-up calls.

Advertise

Give careful thought to your advertising strategy. Much money can be wasted on nonproductive advertising. Advertise in the newspapers, business magazines, and local cable TV. Use many small ads frequently, rather than one large expensive ad. Most find that a listing or modest ad in the Yellow Pages is the best source of customers. The listing also tells the customer you are established in the community. When you get a lead, follow up immediately.

Targeting

A favorite approach is to target your sales. Identify a specific niche that needs your services and organize a marketing effort geared to that niche. Do your homework and study the homes or businesses with the best potential for your service. When it comes to business prospects, don't be afraid of the big ones. Within 6 to 12 months after you have done some smaller accounts, go after the bigger ones. Also, try to find out in advance the name of the executive who will decide if you get their business, such as the facility manager, office manager, or bank vice-president, etc. You may find some have delegated this to their secretaries, but depending on your service, you will do better if you can get to the decision-making person. In the case of residential customers, treat both the woman and man with equal weight.

Next, on your sharp-looking new letterhead, type or have typed a letter introducing you and your service. At the end of your brief letter, say that you will call at a certain time on a certain day next week to see if you can get an appointment (see Figure 2.1). Then be on time! Call exactly when you said you would. Ask for an appointment and then keep it as though the future of your business depended on it. It does. Promptness should be an earmark of all your business appointments. It tells the prospect that you are a person who keeps your word and can be trusted. This principle, too, applies to residential customers. Service

FIGURE 2.1: Letter of Introduction to a Targeted Customer

Acme Service

P.O. Box 2500
Mytown, SC 29000   July 10, 2000

Mr. Robert Jones
ABC Company
P.O. Box 20
Mytown, SC 29000

Dear Mr. Jones:

  As you may know, Acme Service has been providing quality maintenance services to many facilities in this area. I would like to have the opportunity to show you how our services could provide reliable maintenance to your facility and possibly save you money over the present service you are using.

  I will be calling your office for an appointment next Monday morning at 9 AM. If you can give me about ten to fifteen minutes sometime next week, I would appreciate the opportunity to meet you and present what we have for your consideration.

  Thank you for considering this matter.

                                      Michael Smith

people who do not keep appointments leave a bad impression and may well lose the business.

As you make your presentation, emphasize how you operate. Ask if he or she has any areas that need improving in the service they are getting and then ask for an opportunity to bid and improve on the service. As you talk, emphasize the strengths of your service. Identify major sources of complaint and highlight how you are overcoming the problem. Show how your service gives extra attention in these areas. When your prospect talks, be a good listener. Often the prospect will lead you into the area where you need to concentrate.

This targeted approach gets results. Try it.

Referrals or Networking

Even if turned down at first, ask if the homeowner or businessperson knows someone who may need or be interested in your service. Ask any business people you know or with whom you trade if they know any other businesses that need your service. When they give you a suggestion, follow up on it. Be sure to use the name of the businessperson who referred you when you call on the prospect. When you go in, you might say: "Mr. Jones, I'm glad to meet you. I was talking with Mr. Roberts at ABC Corporation the other day and he suggested I might come by to see you. I would like to acquaint you with a program we have that may be of help to you."

> - Cold calls
> - Advertise
> - Target sales
> - Referrals

There are, however, many other approaches beside these suggestions. Some use the telephone or set up a booth at a trade show for homeowners and businesses in the area. The main thing to remember is that you can only grow and achieve your goals in this business if you make the sales calls. So set aside a specific scheduled portion of your time every week for this important part of your business for as long as you are in the business.

Marketing is a critical area of any successful operation. Let this chapter serve as a primer as you start. Expand your understanding of this important part of your business by reading other books on the subject, such as *Power Marketing* by Jody Hornor or *Marketing Mastery* by Stephenson & Otterson (both published by The Oasis Press).

Congratulations! You have found a prospect that wants a price. But how do you go about figuring out how much to charge and preparing a bid? Read on.

How to Bid

"Anybody can win unless there happens to be a second entry."

—George Ade

Before discussing how to bid, it would be good to consider *if* you want to bid on a particular job at all. Some jobs are best left for others. It takes a little time and experience to get to know what jobs are desirable and what jobs you don't want. Sometimes you are better off making a $100 profit at one location than driving to ten locations, knocking yourself out, to finish with only a $10 profit from each job.

To apply this logic to your business, you may want to turn down the opportunity to bid on the jobs that are very small, far away, or spread out among many small branches — unless it is made worth your time. Thus many experienced in the business seek jobs that are centralized rather than spread out over the city, state, or region. They realize that time in transit eats away at profit. Also be wary of the prospect strictly looking for the cheapest price in town. Seek out clients who look for and pay for quality work and you will be in business for a long time.

The Bidding Process

Now let's get down to the bidding process. It consists of two basic steps:

1. Determining the price

2. Making the presentation

Determining the Price

In order to decide what to charge, you would be wise to make a site survey (or what some call a walk-through). This will determine how close you can bid and still show a reasonable gross profit (25 to 45 percent). As you go through the building, be aware of the following items:

- Take notes.

- Estimate the square footage, if applicable.

- Determine the age and condition of the building, buildings, or objects needing your service.

- Access density (For example, if you are to provide a service in an office or home, are the rooms filled with furniture that must be covered, moved, or cleaned or is the space relatively open?)

- Estimate carpeted, tile, or terrazzo square footage, if you will be cleaning any of these.

- Determine hours during which work must be done.

- Note extras or areas to receive special care.

- Determine deadlines you will be required to meet.

- Note environmental considerations.

- Meet the company representative or individual with whom you will have to interface.

There are a number of methods to determine the fair price, but be forewarned. It is like playing the piano — it will take practice to master any of them. Therefore, the wise thing to do on your first few bids is to be conservative and bid on smaller jobs. *This principle is appropriate to all the service businesses in this book.*

Square-Foot System

The first and perhaps easiest system to master is the per-square-foot system. The per-square-foot price range you use is determined by:

1. Your operating costs (labor, supplies, and overhead)

2. Your area (small town or large city)

Suppose you provide a regular weekly service, such as office maintenance or restroom service, and you give a customer a bid of 3.5 cents per square foot per week on a 5,000 square foot facility. This would give you a price of $175 per week, based on daily service 52 weeks a year (be sure to stipulate that in your agreement). The customer would like to get it done cheaper, perhaps by having it done only three times a week. How do you figure it? Simple. Subtract 20 percent from your five-day price. Why only 20 percent instead of 40 percent? Because you will still be cleaning five days worth of dirt, only now you have to do it in three days. Plus there are certain services that were figured in the five-day price that are performed weekly and monthly that will still be included in the price. So the new price is $140 per week. Once again, this principle can be applied to any number of service businesses, particularly those you will provide on a regular basis.

Some service businesses that fit into this category might be office cleaning, carpet cleaning, maid service, restroom service, parking lot cleaning, trash removal, restaurant cleaning (and hood filter cleaning), computer and office machine cleaning, floor maintenance, yacht cleaning, window cleaning, landscaping services, and swimming pool service, to name a few.

This square-foot formula is fairly simple once you get the hang of it. You will need to experiment with it some to get it to work for your operation and your area.

In the beginning you will be understandably nervous about underpricing a job. A little trick you might use on small regular maintenance jobs you are not sure how to price: Offer to do it one time free to give a sample of your work. Some will take you up on it. It will be a gesture of your confidence in your work, it will build goodwill, but the most important thing you will determine is how long it will take to do the job. Say it took you four hours, because you did some "detailing" to impress the customer. That included taking time to do some extra things, or you maybe needed extra time to set up or clean neglected areas. You may estimate that it can easily be done in three hours. You then multiply your hourly worth by three. Say you figure you are worth around $20 per hour by the time you figure your gas, travel time, and insurance. That's $60 per night or $300 per week. It is another simple technique for arriving at a price in the beginning. It may help you now and then until you gain more experience estimating.

Workloading System

Another and more complex method of bidding is being used by a number of successful contractors. It is the workloading system. These contractors determine what their actual cost will be to do a job (as close as they can), and then add their profit on top of it. One successful high-volume cleaning contractor simply adds a 25 percent profit on top of his cost. To illustrate, lets say his job is 50,000 square feet of average office space, and the average employee can clean 3,500 square feet overall per hour. Therefore, it will take 14.28 hours (or about 14 hours) to do the job. Suppose your cost per hour for that employee is $15 (including FICA, insurance, workers' compensation). That would make your cost $214.20 per night or $1,071.00 per week. Add in cleaning supplies, equipment, uniforms, office expenses of approximately 20 percent: $229.40. Now you have your true cost — $1,300.40 per week. Don't forget your profit margin — 25 percent or $422.76 — and you have a total of $1723.16 per week for basic services. A procedure many large contractors use to double-check themselves is to compare the results of the square-foot formula with the workloading formula to be sure they are in the ballpark. Once again, you can apply this formula to any number of service businesses.

Add-Ons

The last time you bought a new car, did the salesperson try to get you to buy the extras rather than just a basic model? Of course. The add-ons affect the profit margin tremendously. That's true in your business too. You will find in the second section of this book many add-ons and how to price them.

One example is a profitable high-volume carpet cleaning business. This can also be an add-on to a maid service or an office cleaning service. Rather than a one-time sale, some companies will let you set up on a scheduled system to maintain their carpeting. You can further add on stain retardant treatment and upholstery and drapery cleaning.

Say you are pricing an office-cleaning contract. Here are five things to consider as add-ons:

1. If you usually provide your service after business hours, would the customer like to have a daytime employee from your company on the job to care for things that come up during the day? (Use the workloading system to price.)

2. Would the customer like the executive offices given special care? (For example, executive restrooms sanitized twice a day?)

3. Would the customer like certain executive offices detailed every night? Or, if you provide security guard service, extra personnel or attention in sensitive areas?

4. Would the customer like an unlimited service available for their lobby, halls, or areas most exposed to public view?

5. Would the customer like an energy-saver program implemented? (One large corporation was able to save nearly $50,000 per year when their outside service implemented this program.) This will be a valuable selling tool that will help you stand above your competition. It simply means getting in and out of the building in a smaller time frame, using a larger crew and training everyone to turn off the lights when they are through with a section. The cost to the customer of this program is nominal (3 to 5 percent of your normal price) when compared to the saving for a large facility.

There are many other profitable add-ons you can implement after you successfully get the bid. Be observant. Find a need and fill it for a price. Doing this, you will take jobs of minimum profit and improve them considerably.

Pricing Supplies

When pricing a job you will almost always include supplies in your service. But there are certain supplies you always want the customer to provide. A few examples: When pricing a lighting service, the customer provides the bulbs and ballasts. In the case of a restroom cleaning, the cost of toilet paper, paper towels, and trash can liners vary greatly from one customer to another, and it is almost impossible to determine when estimating a job. So it is best to have the customer provide these. More details about this will be considered later with individual service businesses. As a general rule, supplies in most service businesses rarely exceed 5 to 10 percent of the total price.

Again, careful shopping will pay off for you in higher profits. As you grow you will find suppliers will give you a greater discount. Keep comparing and testing new products. As industries progress, newer techniques and products can do the job faster and better. Take advantage of them.

Further help with the bidding process is in the Section 2 of this book. This information will be specific to the individual service business.

Now that you have estimated what price you want, what's next? You will want to present it to your prospect.

The Proposal

"He that promises too much means nothing."

— Thomas Fuller (1732)

Your proposal is your honest estimation of what you can do and for how much.

Proposals vary from simple to very complex, depending on the size and nature of the account for which you design it. Some are the size of books. Some customers may be impressed by this, although most prefer a get-to-the-point proposal. Some contractors even include a copy of the proposed contract with the proposal. Not a bad idea. It will often circumvent the problems you may encounter in negotiating details, or discourage the customer from drawing up his or her own contract (which will almost always favor the customer).

As we look at this important part of securing new business, we want to emphasize the most important part of any proposal, whether it is short or long — it represents you. So far, from the initial contact and visit, the walk-through and results of checking your references, your prospective customer has been sizing you up. The customer is trying to decide whether you or the company you represent is capable and competent enough to provide the service. It is, after all, a matter of trust. Some service businesses require that you have the keys or at least access to a facility worth hundreds of thousands or even millions of dollars.

Before the prospective customer ever sees your proposal, the key to its success and acceptance is your early impression. Your goal should be to convey to this prospect the impression that you are honest and sincere. Your conduct and demeanor through these negotiations should build this image. That is why your appearance and the overall impression of your sales materials is so important. Conducting yourself in a professional manner may be the most effective part of the whole sales process — indeed often more important than the best price.

One book on the subject asserts that customers will pay up to 10 percent more to the right service. Look at the following example to illustrate the point. You go to a seafood restaurant and order a fried flounder fillet. It comes with a salad and baked potato. The cost for this meal may be $9.95. You tip the wait-person 15 percent and think you may have been too generous. Or you go to another seafood restaurant with dimmed lights, soft music, cloth napkins and tablecloths. You order the same dinner for $18.95. You tip the waitperson, dressed in white shirt and tie, 18 percent and wonder if it was enough. The point is you want your company to be perceived as a class act worth everything you are asking and more. Therefore, you must present yourself as the right service for your customer's needs.

Once you have conveyed the right impression you need to decide which type of proposal to use: the short proposal or the long proposal.

The Short Proposal

A short proposal will be used most often on smaller accounts. It can be adjusted in wording for most of the service businesses in this book. You can do this in two ways: (1) a simple proposal, or (2) a proposal that includes an agreement or contract. (Most customers prefer calling it an agreement rather than contract. As mentioned earlier, the word contract makes some customers nervous, although basically they are the same thing.) There are some very nice preprinted forms of a short proposal available from local office supply stores, as well as computer programs. (See Chapter 10.) Figure 4.1 is an example of a short proposal. Study the basic layout so you can easily convert the form to your service.

FIGURE 4.1: The Short Proposal

Proposal

(Your Name, Address & Phone)   For: (Customer's Name, Address & Phone)

ITEM Other	Daily	Weekly	Monthly	Other	ITEM	Daily	Weekly	Monthly	

OTHER REQUIREMENTS:

_____

_____

_____

Supplies will be provided by:

Total Cost of Service $ _____ per _____

Service to begin on _____ This agreement expires _____

By _____   By _____
            Contractor   Customer

Date _____   Date _____

(This is only a sample to show what information may be included — not a legal document)

The Long Proposal

The long proposal is generally used for large accounts. It is hard to find one of these ready-made. You may need to consult with a lawyer to make sure you protect yourself and your company from liability.

The long proposal will be used when you meet with the facility manager (or the equivalent). In a larger facility like this, often you will be asked to leave the proposal for consideration when the manager meets with other members of the company. Therefore, since you probably will not be able to meet face to face with those who make the final decision, what you put in this proposal must present you and your company in the best possible way. It is very important that you provide the facility manager with everything he or she needs. You also hope your first impression will cause the facility manager to promote you to the others in that room.

The following are some ideas for your proposal:

- Put it in a nice presentation folder (obtainable at most office supply stores).

- Attach a business card to the outside of the front cover.

- Type a brief letter on your letterhead explaining your desire to service their facility and why you believe your company is the best for the job (one to two paragraphs are plenty). Address it to the attention of the facility manager.

- Include a typed list of your references (other customers) as well as bank and insurance companies.

- Provide copies, if required, proof of your applicable insurances (workers' compensation, liability, etc.) for the job. Your insurance company should be able to provide you with extra copies of these, or make photocopies for this purpose.

- Include a complete schedule of what you are going to do and when you are going to do it. Detail is important in this type of proposal. Many of your competitors may be offering the same thing for about the same price, but the customer may choose your bid simply because you listed much more detail. A sample of such a work schedule is provided later in the book.

- Include the basic price on the same page as the work schedule (a nice touch) or on a page of its own.

- Add a page that lists available options and how much they will cost. (Often it is nice to mention that this price or option is available "only to our contract customers.")

- Include a copy of your proposed contract (or agreement). Figure 4.2 is a sample suggested contract. Fill it out with that specific account in mind, but don't sign it yet. On larger accounts the customer's lawyers may want a few changes.

Finally, when and if all goes well and the prospective customer returns the final contract or agreement to you, take it to your lawyer for consideration. Keep in mind, what we have presented here is just a sample. Due to the variance of the laws, you are wise if you consult with a business lawyer in your area — especially when considering a large job. But again, there are definite advantages to having a standard contract and including it in your presentation. It will increase your control of the job.

FIGURE 4.2: A Sample Suggested Contract for a Long Proposal

YOUR STATE

YOUR COUNTY

CONTRACT

THIS AGREEMENT, made and entered into this ____ day of _____, ____, by and between _____, hereinafter referred to as "Customer", and _____, hereinafter referred to as "Contractor".

WITNESSETH:

WHEREAS, the Customer desires to arrange for services as hereinafter set forth;

WHEREAS, the contractor desires to provide such service for Customer as hereinafter set forth;

NOW, THEREFORE, in accordance with the mutual covenants herein contained, the parties agree as follows:

1. *Employment.* The Customer hereby employs the Contractor and the Contractor hereby accepts such employment upon the terms and conditions herein set forth;

2. *Relationship Between Parties.* Contractor is employed as an independent contractor for the purpose of performing services as enumerated herein by Customer.

FIGURE 4.2: continued

Employees of the Contractor are not employees of the Customer.

3. *Term.* The term of the Contract shall begin on the effective date set forth above and shall continue until terminated as herein provided.

4. *Duties.* Contractor will provide services to the Customer as follows or in accordance with a corresponding Work Schedule:

   _____

   _____

5. *Compensation.* For all services rendered, compensation shall be paid by Customer as follows: The services herein designated shall be performed on a ____-day schedule per Schedule A at the rate of $_____ per week.

   If more or less service is requested or required, the compensation rate shall be increased or decreased prorata in accordance with the rate applicable to the particular premises.

   Any increase or decrease in work to be completed in accordance with the attached Schedule will be renegotiated, and all such negotiations on behalf of the Contractor must be done only with and by _____.

6. *Special Services.* Any services requested which are not on the normal work schedule will be billed in accordance with the mutual written agreement between the designated Customer representative, _____, and the designated Contractor representative, _____.

7. *Payment.* All payments to be made under this contract shall be as follows: Contractor will provide a written weekly invoice to Customer for services rendered. Said invoice is due upon receipt and payable within ten (10) days of receipt. Payments are based on a fifty-two (52) week calendar year.

8. *Supplies.* [Stipulate here what supplies each party must provide.]

9. *Equipment.* [Stipulate here what equipment each party must provide.]

10. *Insurance.* Contractor agrees to maintain, at its own expense, insurance in the amount of $_____ (XXXXXX Dollars) to protect Contractor and Customer from any claim for damage to person or property or for injury to any employee of Contractor while Contractor or its employees are providing any services under the terms of the Contract.

11. *Contract Price Revisions.* Contractor retains the right to review the Contract price every ninety days in order to make any necessary adjustment for inflation and cost of living index. In the event that a price revision is necessary, Contractor will give

FIGURE 4.2: continued

Customer written notice of the proposed price revision ninety (90) days prior to the effective date of said price revision. If the parties are unable to reach a written agreement concerning the price revision, then either party may terminate this Contract by giving a written thirty-days' notice to the other party.

12. *Termination.* In addition to the Contract termination as provided above, either party may terminate this Contract for any reason by giving the other party written thirty-days' notice.

13. *Notice.* All notice required to be given under the terms of this Contract shall be in writing, shall be effective upon receipt, and shall be delivered to the addressee in person or mailed by certified mail, return receipt requested, as follows:

If to the Customer, address to: If to the Contractor, address to:

_____   _____

_____   _____

_____   _____

14. *Amendments.* This Contract may be amended only by written agreement between the parties hereto. All amendments are to be approved and renegotiated on behalf of the Contractor only by and with _____.

15. *Captions.* The captions contained in this Contract are for convenience only and shall in no manner be construed as part of this Contract.

16. *Counterparts.* This Contract is executed in two (2) counterparts, each of which shall be deemed an original and together shall constitute one in the same agreement, with one executed counterpart being retained by each party hereto.

IN WITNESS WHEREOF, Customer has hereunto caused its corporate name to be signed by its duly authorized officer, and Contractor have hereunto set their hands and seals, all being done in duplicate originals, with one original being delivered to each party as of the _____ day of _____, ____.

_____   By:_____
CUSTOMER

_____   By:_____
CONTRACTOR

(This contract is presented as a sample only to show what items might be included in a contract. Since laws vary from state to state, for your own protection, legal help is strongly suggested.

The Boardroom Presentation

Though rare, occasionally you will be asked to come into a meeting with the "brass" when they are considering bids for service and make a personal presentation. Other services, such as secretarial or temporary employment services, may require such a presentation. Should this happen, don't panic; put on your best suit, and look sharp. Have copies of your basic proposal to give to each person in the room. Don't let speaking to a group intimidate you. Look mostly at the person in charge and occasionally move your eyes to look at other individuals in the room for a sentence or two. Present your information in a business-like manner, and don't take too much time. Ask if anyone has any questions, answer them honestly, thank them for their time, and take your leave.

Customer Education

Probably you will be bidding against others. The competition may quote a really low price to the customer. But are they comparing apples to apples? Will the competitor be doing everything you are offering for your price? Indeed, you may be bidding against someone who will promise everything and then deliver very little. Frankly, it is sometimes hard to deal with dishonest competitors. But because of your first impression you have established yourself as a person of integrity, delivering what you promise. You will also have the advantage that you have put in writing everything you are going to do and when you are going to do it. This will make you stand out from your competitors and will educate your customer as to what your bid truly represents compared to other prices. (If you get the bid and begin work in the facility, writing everything out will also protect you. Sometimes the customer forgets what was agreed upon, balking if you bill for an added service, thinking it should be included. Having everything in writing is a protection and can save you from disagreements.)

Now let's look at some more basics about doing the work.

Equipment

"The machine yes the machine —- never wastes anybody's time — never watches the foreman—never talks back."

—Carl Sandburg (1936)

Now that you have some customers to help pay the bills, it's time to talk about equipment. What? You mean you should go out and try and get accounts before you even own any equipment?

That's right. That is why this chapter is placed after the ones about getting the business, bidding, and the proposal. It is, of course, up to you as to how you want to approach this, but many have run their businesses on a "minimum-risk" policy with good results. The premise is: Don't buy a piece of equipment until you have the business to pay for it. After all, only after you secure an account will you know what you will need in equipment and supplies.

What if you live in an area where equipment is not readily available and it takes a long time to ship to you? What if you order the equipment you need for that new job and it is back ordered? Don't panic. In most cases, the first few jobs can be done with rental equipment.

Of course, you should do your homework on equipment before you call on customers. Then you will know what is available, how much it will cost, and how long it will take to get it delivered. Also, the cost of the equipment will be a factor in your bid for the job.

What Do I Need?

What will you need, and how much will it cost? In order to answer that, you need to look at two different approaches to starting your business.

Although the days of "mom and pop" operations seem to be disappearing, most established services started that way. Realistically, most people start out in business with a limited amount of money on hand to invest in their idea, as in Approach A. On the other hand, if you have or can borrow start-up capital, then you can take advantage of Approach B.

Approach A

Before you begin to buy a lot of new equipment, you will do well to remember one important fact: In the service business industry, you are selling yourself — that is, your ability and performance. Driving up with a lot of new equipment will not impress a customer nearly as much as quality work, even if you use old equipment. Indeed, driving up with all new equipment may tell the customer you have never done this before. He will lose confidence in you from the start.

As you begin your service business, look at what you may already have. Here are a few examples.

If you are starting a landscaping business, look around your home. Do you already have a decent lawn mower, maybe even a rider? You probably have a power string trimmer too and one of those leaf blowers. Look in your basement or tool shed and you will probably find most basic tools: rake, shovel, wheelbarrow, grass seed spreader, etc.

What you don't have, you may want to buy locally. Shop around. Don't feel you need to buy "heavy duty professional" equipment from a specialty supplier for the trade. Sometimes what you need can be found at a local discount store and at a better price too. If, however, you run into a job requiring specialized equipment, you can always rent it until you have the volume to justify buying.

Next, you are probably thinking of a truck to transport your equipment to the job. Well, that's a real need. If you don't have a pickup truck or van available already, perhaps a used one can be found at a reasonable price. Or you could look into buying a utility trailer and use your present car to pull it to the job. That would also save you considerably in insurance and mechanical maintenance for a second vehicle.

The same principles apply to any service business you pursue. The one exception would be a window-cleaning service. This is one business that requires you use the best squeegees and other equipment on the market to do a quality job in a minimum of time. However, the start-up cost for this business is so low, you can afford to buy the best.

There are a few excellent sources of used equipment. Read the classified ads. You can sometimes find what you need just slightly used. Rental shops sometimes sell used equipment. If you are looking for things like buffers, heavy-duty vacuums, or carpet-cleaning equipment, you may find these items in the back of an older department store. Often they have not been used for some time, and the manager would be glad get a few bucks for it.

Approach B

This approach is for the entrepreneur with some financial backing who wants to approach this endeavor first-class. Don't go out and buy all kinds of equipment until you know what kinds of jobs you will obtain and exactly what you will need. The following example explains a few basics.

You want to start a contract janitorial service. If you were starting on a budget, you might buy one good vacuum or even use the one you have at home. But you know you will soon need more, so invest in a couple of powerful upright vacuums (at least 12 to 18 AMPs motor power).

You will need a floor buffer. Look for a used one if you are on a budget, or invest in a new one. The range in cost is tremendous, but a good buffer is a solid investment and one that will last a long time if you properly maintain it. Here again, the type of business you get will determine the type of buffer you will need. They vary as to the block size, rotating speed, and whether electric or propane powered. Each has its application.

So you want a new truck, too? Fine, if you can afford it. However, consider this suggestion: If you have some money left over, save it to live on while you are getting started. If you still feel you need a truck, you may find a good used one. Once again, the type of business you pursue can influence this decision. A heavily used vehicle, such as a garbage truck or parking lot sweeper, will get enough use to justify a purchase of a new one. Generally speaking, most businesses start out with used equipment and move up to new when they see the client base begin to grow. Having the name of your company painted on a work vehicle new or used would be a plus. You could also have magnetic signs made up for when you use your family vehicle.

Eventually you will add all sorts of equipment to your inventory. But always be conservative in purchasing new equipment. Try to make all purchases on a cash basis. It will keep your stress level down.

Perhaps this approach seems conservative, but wouldn't you rather put the extra money in your pocket than in equipment that sits in the back room of your office?

Either Way You Go ...

For either approach, allow some extra room for things not foreseen. Accounts will vary as to their needs. If you desire or need to start up your operation at a more intense level than listed above, you need a consultant. It will be money well spent if you use one to guide you through the difficult and challenging start-up process.

Your local community college probably offers a night course designed to help people like you who are trying to get a business off the ground. Why not check with your local college and see what they offer?

During my career, I once advised a woman who was a single parent and wanted my help getting started. I said, "Don't be afraid of the big jobs." I made that statement because most people start with small jobs that show little or no profit. I encouraged her to aim a little higher. She aimed high all right; she called a few weeks later asking for help in figuring a price on an office complex that would be the envy of even the largest, well-established service business. Now that's positive thinking, but not really the ideal way to start off. Large contracts make large demands and expect experienced people to handle their account. If possible, give yourself some time to understand the basics of the business and then start to go after the really large accounts.

If you land a larger contract from the start or down the road, you will soon be dealing with the need for selecting and hiring personnel. This is the subject of the next chapter.

6

Personnel

"He who considers his work beneath him will be above doing it well."

—Alexander Chase, Perspectives (1966)

You have landed a nice, fat $55,000 a year account. Nice start. Picture your first day or night on the job. You and some of your relatives pull up to the location. As you all pile out of the car, you are excited. You are finally on your way. Not yet. What's wrong?

Image

How do you all look? Old grubby work clothes? It is obvious that no one in the group knows what he is doing. That's the mistake a lot of your competitors make. Be different. Before you show up that first time, go and get some professional uniforms. Have them all the same color, with your company name on them. Also, don't be afraid of using a bright color. If you do some work at night, such as parking lot service or cleaning, you may face the all-too-common scenario when police officers or security guards are surprised when coming around a corner in the middle of the night to suddenly come upon one of your employees. How tragic it would be if one of them were shot by accident. Their easily identified bright uniforms may literally save their lives. This is particularly important if your people will be in high-risk or high-security areas late at

A client was working near a sheriff's office one night after a big drug raid. When the deputies heard noise outside, they ran out with guns drawn. His bright red uniform shirt could be seen in the darkness and immediately identified him as one of the "good guys."

night. The cost is about $25 each for shirts or smocks, including your company name and personal name of the employee sewn on. This is well worth it for the look they will give you. While you are at it, add some security badges. This will give a nice touch to everyone's appearance — some accounts may require it.

How does your equipment look as you carry it into the customer's building? Clean and polished? Good. Try to keep it that way. Require yourself and your employees to leave their equipment clean after every shift and keep the supply closets, any work vehicles, lawn mowers, and anything else immaculate. This could put you another step out in front of your competitors.

Now, what about hiring all your relatives and your buddies? That can be good — good if you invite the ones that know how to work hard, can be trusted, and can take direction from you. Or it can be bad — bad if they are looking for an easy deal. Hire with your head and not your heart. (Many of us have learned the hard way that it is better to make a friend out of an employee than make an employee out of a friend or a relative.)

Finding Good Help

This is an extremely important part of your business. Most service businesses are labor-intensive. The most valuable investments you will make in this industry are not equipment — but people. Select them like your success depends on them, because it does.

From the first employee you hire, follow fair, legal hiring and employment practices and then stick to them. Take some time to learn the fundamentals of the laws on this. Then as your company grows, continue to increase the depth of your knowledge, or delegate it to a trusted employee.

You will want to put your personnel policies in writing as you develop. As your business reaches some size, you will even want to develop your own personnel policy manual. The book, *A Company Policy & Personnel Workbook,* by Ardella Ramey and Carl Sniffen (published by PSI Research/Oasis Press) can be helpful. There are even some computer programs to aid you. The following should be considered when looking for employees.

- Have everyone fill out an application. Personally interview each employee. After you have hired someone, you may wish to prepare a file folder to keep copies of all forms and any other information about this person while in your employ.

- Check everyone's background back seven years or more. The very nature of most service businesses requires that you can trust your employees.

- Have everyone get a basic physical and drug test. Shop for a doctor who will give you the best price for this service. Have the employee sign an agreement to recover the cost of the physical if they leave after a few weeks. (See Figure 6.1.)

- Pay the employees a little more than your competitors.

- If the newly-hired employees are working out and you want to keep them, commend them well whenever they deserve it, and pay them a fair and progressive wage.

- Consider a Probationary Employee Agreement (Figure 6.2) to protect you should an employee not be able to do the job. Hiring and firing is not as easy as it used to be. The laws now require considerable documentation and a number of warnings before you can actually fire someone. Thus, hiring on a trial or temporary basis may protect you from a lawsuit. After the employee has proved capable of the job, you can then offer a permanent position.

- Look for husband and wife teams for smaller accounts. These often prove to be reliable and tend to stay with your company longer.

- Above all, look for honest people. It is far more important than experience. Be careful not to discriminate by sex, race, or creed or your lawyer will own your business!

Although you are going to be hiring people who will mostly be doing physical work, disabled individuals are not to be overlooked. Much depends on the type of disablility. For example, if the person is in a wheelchair, he or she may be trained to handle the office end of your business. If missing limbs, they can still perform many of the physical duties required. A truck rigged for a disabled driver can be used for delivery services, parking lot sweeping, and trash service. If you are patient and willing to take the time to train them, hiring disabled employees may be one of the best investments you make. Not to be overlooked are the tax incentives that are offered. Check them out.

FIGURE 6.1: Sample Employee Agreement

Sample Employee Agreement

As a new employee of Acme Service, I understand that I could be dismissed at the discretion of Acme Service. I further understand that, if I should leave this employment for whatever reason, I am required to turn in the following items:

1. The uniforms provided by the company.

2. Personal picture ID badge

3. Any keys issued to me.

If I fail to return any of these items, I understand that my last check will be withheld until all items are turned in to the office.

A pre-employment physical examination, including drug screening, by the company doctor is required. The company will pay for this examination. However, I understand that, should I leave this employment within 60 days, the cost of the physical will be deducted from my last paycheck.

I hereby give permission for the company to do a complete background check, due to the often-sensitive customer areas and nature of the work I will be performing.

In addition, it is agreed and understood that there will be no smoking or drinking of alcoholic beverages on the job. Also, I understand that if "off the job" drinking of alcohol affects either my punctuality or performance, it is reason for dismissal.

By affixing my signature to this form I indicate that I have read and agree with the above conditions.

_____
Signature of Employee

_____
Date

This is a sample — a compilation of some agreements used in various states. State laws differ and labor laws often undergo change. Check with your attorney or Employment Security Commission.

FIGURE 6.2: Probationary Employee Agreement

Probationary Employee Agreement

I, _____, as an employee of Acme Service acknowledge that I am hired for a 30-day probationary period. I understand that after that time, if I fail to meet the standards of Acme Service, I can be dismissed.

During that 30-day period I will be rated on my job performance, punctuality, grooming, and attitude.

Employee Copy   Signed: _____

                                  Date:_____

Probationary Employee Agreement

I, _____, as an employee of Acme Service acknowledge that I am hired for a 30-day probationary period. I understand that after that time, if I fail to meet the standards of Acme Service, I can be dismissed.

During that 30-day period I will be rated on my job performance, punctuality, grooming, and attitude.

Company Copy   Signed: _____

                                  Date:_____

Be sure employee signs both copies. As with other forms in this text, we accept no legal responsibility — Check laws in your area with Employment Security Commission.

Where Do I Find These People?

As we have already discussed, you could first look for help with some of your family or relatives, if they are qualified. Other places to look are:

- Classified ads

- State employment offices

- University or community college campuses

- Handicapped organizations — there are a number of ways to employ handicapped people.

- Referrals. Sometimes current employees will refer others to you. But be cautious of this avenue. You may get some good employees if they are qualified, but if you have to fire them, you also may lose or affect the attitude of the one that referred them to you.)

- Develop a "B" list from current or even new employees hired on a trial basis. This group is to provide help to cover absentees or last minute rush jobs. Some former employees may also agree to fill in on occasion.

Now that you have the employees you need, what else should you consider?

Training

The next chapter will devote itself to an abbreviated training program that you can use to teach your employees the fundamentals. The various trade associations in your business offer more extensive and specialized training programs for you and your employees. Be sure you take the program yourself, as well as seeing that your employees take it. They will respect you for that. In fact, always set the example. Show them you are not afraid to get your hands dirty.

Keeping Track of Hours

Keeping track of hours worked by employees is difficult in some service businesses. If your business requires having people on a number of different jobs, having a time clock or trusted supervisor on hand is not always practical. Many use a simple time sheet, such as the one in Figure 6.3. You or your supervisor should check it each week for accuracy. It is a valuable tool for two reasons:

1. It gives you an inexpensive way to keep track of your employees' hours.

2. Experience has taught that if employees are dishonest or becoming dishonest, they will often reveal this tendency by stealing time from you. It would be preferable to deal with them for stealing from you rather than from the customer, possibly losing you a large contract. The time sheet can ultimately reveal a lot more about your employee than the hours worked.

Of course, on very large accounts you may choose to use time clocks. There is even a call-in computer program for keeping track of your employees' time.

FIGURE 6.3: Weekly Time Report

Weekly Time Report

Pay Date: _____

	Start	Stop	Start	Stop	Day Total
Monday					
Tuesday					
Wednesday					
Thursday					
Friday					
Saturday					
Sunday					
TOTAL					

Employee Signature: _____

Supervisor Signature: _____

Out of every 4 hours, take a 10-minute break.
For every 8 hours, take a 30-minute lunch break.
Break times are not to be counted with work time.

CHAPTER

7

Training

"Much effort, much prosperity."

—Euripides, *The Suppliant Women* (c. 421 B.C.), tr. Frank W. Jones

A few years ago a company in North Carolina began to franchise. They did one thing and they did it very well. They cleaned toilets. They are now an international company. If you want to be successful at something, learn how from someone who does it better than anyone else. Study what they do and how they do it. If you wanted to start a successful restroom service, you would benefit from a careful study of this North Carolina company's approach. Whether you are cleaning, landscaping, painting, or providing any type of service, observe the techniques of those who have succeeded and adapt them to your business.

A successful owner-operator in business is probably one of the most technically educated people you will meet. There are new and better products and procedures coming out all the time. One must keep up-to-date through constant learning. Through trade magazines, books, videos and seminars, the owner upgrades his or her education. Surprised?

From the very first job, you will want to begin to educate yourself and whoever helps you. As you learn, set goals and standards of quality work. When you reach that standard, hang on to it and work hard to see that your employees follow your example. This means, then, at the early stage of your business you will be a salesperson, a manager, a purchasing agent, a personnel director, and a teacher.

The key to a most effective training program for your business is that *you* should design it and tailor it to the demands of your client base. Using videos, textbooks, chalkboards (or whiteboards), and demonstrations, you will want to help your employees perform well on the job.

The first thing that you and your employees want to learn in your business is *motion economy*. The following example explains how this concept is important.

Recently, when on a large construction site, I was watching a line of about ten bricklayers put up a brick wall. The younger bricklayers were impressively fast as they rapidly laid their brick. I thought, "I wish I had their energy." But then I noticed an elderly brick mason down at the end of the line; his name was Jim Hardy. This brick mason from Aiken, South Carolina, has been laying brick for over 60 years. He was laying the corners as well as putting bricks down on the line. The corners take more time than the line, and yet he was keeping up with the young guys. How did he do it? *Motion economy.*

He had learned over the years how to make every move count. When Jim reached down and scooped up cement with his trowel, he got all he needed to "butter" and lay that brick. While the younger guys were reaching down for cement two or three times, he did it once and accomplished the same thing.

How do we apply that principle to your business? Many ways. When you do a job, try to do it right the first time. In the beginning get the right moves and techniques down and speed will come automatically. The following are some examples.

- When you are bringing equipment and supplies from the supply closet or work truck, try to do it in as few trips as possible. It may be practical to use a cart or carryall — even a box will do — so that you can make only one or two trips. (This is a very important procedure on a large job.) When you teach employees this principle you can greatly affect your profit.

- Whether you are cleaning something in a room or painting, start working to the right or left of the doorway and work in a complete circle around the room. Put your supplies or cart as close to the center of the room as possible. Work from the top down. Do your high work first and then work down. Carry something with you for disposing of any trash or debris.

- Take note of little things: Make a mental note of where things were before you move anything and be sure to replace them there. Get into the habit: As you put down a tool, pick up another for the next job. Before you leave a room or area, inspect your work. Look for missed details or areas that may be a cause for complaint.

- There are aprons that hold supplies and belts that do the same. These can help you master motion economy. Read the trade journals — they are always advertising new innovative gadgets that can help you.

Also, as you train people, develop a "safety first" program. Your customers and employees will respect you for it and your insurance rates could actually go down. Create or buy "how to" posters outlining how you expect certain tasks to be performed. Post them in a place where your employees will see them. (An example is in the chapter on Office Cleaning.) You can use them to teach new employees the basics and to serve as reminders to old employees. As you grow, you will have to train substitute workers on short notice, as well as constantly train new workers. When you train, the first assignment should be to carefully read these charts. Besides technique, these also help to reinforce the high standards you wish to maintain, which will not only set the standard for the employee you are training, but put you ahead of your competition.

There is much more you and your employees need to know. Use training manuals (a number are listed at the back of the book), videos, and memos. But of all the teaching aids available, remember — the most effective and valuable one is you. Live, breathing people like you do the best one-on-one training, both verbally and by example. Someday you may have others do this training for you. Just be sure that you have trained them and that they teach your standards.

> *Consider the postage stamp my son. It secures success through its ability to stick to one thing till it gets there.*
>
> — Josh Billings

In your written agreement with your customer, be sure to establish how often you will provide your service. Then make sure your employees understand just what the customer wants and has agreed to pay for. Why? Customers often see if they can persuade employees to throw in an extra service while they are there. Some services, such as regular cleaning services, require some things done more frequently than others. Be sure this is clear to your employee — something in writing, whether on a chart or an issued worksheet.

Another item often overlooked, as you perfect your technique and enlarge your business with employees, is to train by demonstrating, rather than telling. You would be surprised to know how many times you explain something in what seems to you to be perfectly clear terms. Then when the employee gets on the job, he or she does something entirely different. The problem is communication. You said one thing; the employee heard something else. So the visual effect of demonstrating the technique will have a much greater impact. You may want to then have the employee follow up by demonstrating the same procedure, to be sure he or she understands and can do what you want. Then you can identify problems before he or she is on the job. In addition, in all your work you strive for consistency. So be sure you teach each new employee the exact same techniques.

Other Areas

There are many other areas your training must cover. Don't try to cover it all at once. Remember, when it comes to teaching another person anything, it can be like trying to fill a leaky bucket with water. Make it clear to them up front that training will be an ongoing part of their job, and see to it that it is. If you see someone not responding to your training because he or she feels he has all the answers, then shop for a replacement. It is hard to teach someone who knows everything — anything!

In the beginning see that your employees understand good basics and will try to do their job as though they owned the company. That could happen, you know. Many former employees have been made partners or bought into the company.

How to Treat Your Customer

When on a job, your employees may come in contact with your customer and/or the customer's employees. In fact, when your job takes you into a large complex, a good facility manager will make it a point to walk around the facility or grounds now and then for the express purpose of meeting and talking with your employees.

Emphasize to your workers that, when they are there on the job, they are the company representatives. They should be friendly, greet the client in a friendly manner, and maintain a brief, professionally-oriented conversation. In other words, they should answer any questions the customer may ask, with certain important limitations. This is important in residential work as well as commercial.

Your employees may be asked how they would do something related to the work they are doing. Sometimes the customer is just being friendly, engaging in small talk. However, if asked questions about the contract, money, or other sensitive subjects, train them to say they will contact you and you will be happy to help the client in any way you can. Be sure your employees know that you expect them to stay out of your customer's personal matters, company politics, cliques, and gossip. Their friendly, personable way of dealing with the customer is another way to set your company apart from your competition. It may not be easy for every employee to grasp the importance of this concept, but it will be a great incentive if they know doing this well will be reflected in their paycheck, as well as be a consideration in future promotions.

You can find a number of books and training courses listed in the Appendix. They can help implement these suggestions. A few final thoughts you will want to include in your training program.

- Insist on good grooming. Your employees must look sharp, be clean, and smell clean.

- Teach motion economy and be thorough, efficient.

- Teach them to perform their own on-the-job inspections before leaving a job. (You will want to drop by occasionally to inspect.)

- For inside services especially, tell your employees not to do anything on the job that is unprofessional or could create a misunderstanding. An example of this is: Never sit down on a customer's furniture (particularly upholstered), behind a customer's desk, or open any drawers or cabinets for any reason. There have been some nightmare experiences of employees who have innocently done this, and they as well as their employers suffered terrible consequences.

- Read and follow the work schedule at all times so as not to compromise the terms of your contract or work agreement.

- Help your employees realize it is unprofessional to complain about their work to the customer or fellow employees. Have an open door policy and encourage all workers to come to you at any time with a problem or complaint.

- Encourage your employees to be proud to be one of the best workers for "the most professional service in town." In that respect, pride can be a healthy emotion. When a worker demonstrates professionalism and skill, use that person to help you train others. Groom him or her to become a supervisor.

So now you have a good training program and are ready to go. But are you insured?

Insurance

"Insurance, n. An ingenious modern game of chance in which the player is permitted to enjoy the comfortable conviction that he is beating the man who keeps the table."

—Ambrose Bierce, (1881–1911)

Insurance is something we are glad to have when we need it, but we all hope we never need it. Most service businesses require you or your people to work around, in, or on other people's property. That first time you or someone working with you runs the company truck into a tree or a buffer into a $1,500 mahogany desk (or worse yet, another person), you will understand why you need insurance.

There are many mom and pop operators with no insurance at all. They choose to take the risks. Today they are big risks, particularly if you own a home or have any assets to speak of. One successful lawsuit by a customer or employee could destroy you. Moreover, insurance becomes an absolute necessity if you move on to the level of large accounts. On the plus side, to show a prospective client that you are insured for liability and bonded adds a level of credibility to your company. You could even include a listing of your coverage and limits as part of your sales manual.

You will not need to have most of these insurances in the beginning if you start out on your own. They are briefly covered here to give you a basic understanding of them.

A warning about liability insurance: It does not insure the quality of your work. This coverage has specific limitations. Learn what those limits are in your state with your particular policy.

Liability

This type of insurance covers you for accidents while you or your employees are on the job. For example: While working in the home or office of a customer, you knock over and break a lamp or computer.

With all insurances, get prices from three different agents. It will be worth your time to shop competitively. You will no doubt find a healthy spread in pricing for similar coverage. As you start out, you may wish to get at least a $100,000 liability policy. For a small operation, it may cost as little as $150 per year. Expect that to climb as you grow.

Bonding

Bonding insurance provides protection to your customer against theft by you or one of your employees.

Some insurance agents will admit that this is a joke. How can you insure honesty? Furthermore, in many cases, how can you absolutely prove dishonesty? Businesses lose billions of dollars a year in the United States due to employee theft. It is in this sad climate the honest operator must try to survive. But bonding gives your prospective client some superficial confidence in your company, and it is not that expensive to get. A small operation might spend another $100 or so a year for this coverage.

Workers' Compensation

This insurance compensates any workers you may hire for any on-the-job injuries. Many states only require you to have this if you have four or more employees. When you start to use it, shop carefully. There are some states that have a mandatory arrangement, so that you must buy this insurance from the state. The cost will be based on an experience rating. The less claims you have, the lower your cost will be. This is one more reason to practice a safety-first policy. Let your agent know your safety program. It could help.

Unemployment Insurance

This insurance provides protection to any employees should they be laid off. It will not, however, cover you personally unless you are incorporated and are an employee of the corporation.

Much like workers' compensation, you are required by law to provide this protection for them when you take on employees. You will need to contact your state Employment Security Commission. There will probably be a local office in your county or city. As with workers' compensation, the rate you will have to pay is based on experience — the fewer layoffs you have, the lower your rate will become. However, you must obtain this through the state agency, and they will provide you with the forms you need. There is also a percentage that goes to the federal government. This is figured and paid much like the other payroll taxes you will be handling, which will be discussed further in the next chapter.

Health Insurance

This insurance covers the health coverage costs for you and your employees, as well as family members. To say it can be expensive is an understatement these days.

If you are moonlighting as you start this business and you have group insurance at your day job — great! However, as you develop the business, you will ultimately have to consider this vital insurance. There are group plans available for the self-employed. Look around for them. It may be wise to use a high deductible. Cost can be as little as $50 per month for a college student working through school (although many are covered by their parents' plan as long as they are in school). On the other end is the cost for a mature small operation, which could be $450 a month or more for a husband and wife.

Group coverage can sometimes be found with professional groups or co-ops. If your business grows to have enough employees seeking coverage (usually about ten) you can purchase group insurance coverage. This can bring down the cost somewhat, but, as the employer, you usually will have to contribute at least 50 percent of the employees' premium.

Other Insurance

There are, of course, many other insurances besides these basic five. You may need to look into one of the following:

- personal life insurance
- equipment insurance
- vehicle insurance (for that truck)
- bid bonding
- disability income insurance
- performance bonding

As you can see, insurance can cost you 10 percent (more or less) of your gross income. Shop carefully in order to keep this percentage as low as possible. Look for more than a good price. Shop with a reputable insurance company and select local agents with good reputations.

At this point you are beginning to see that you will not be able to keep all that money you make. You are going to have to spend a lot of money, too. How are you going to keep track of it so that you can be sure there is something left for you?

You already know the answer. You need to learn to keep accurate records. If you are like most, you don't like paperwork. However, a practical system is a must, and it can be simple or complex. Good bookkeeping techniques are next.

Keeping the Books

"Let all things be done decently and in order."

— *Bible* 1 Corinthians 14:40

For most service businesses just starting out, keeping the books might only entail being sure you have a record of all the money you take in and what you spend. The difference is your profit. This could take maybe an hour a week, tops. Then as your business grows it may mean spending one morning a week. Many ask a family member who is a good recordkeeper to take care of this task. By that time you have a few employees. Then the weekly routine would include taking the receipts for the week to the bank, paying the bills, and making out the payroll. The next step might be setting up an office out of the home and hiring a part-time secretary. The workload will probably grow to full-time before long. You get the picture. But the plus side is, the paperwork load grows along with the business and thus it should not be overwhelming; the income growth will take some of the pain away.

Rule 1
Keep the records and money for your business separate from personal records and money.

Strict discipline in this area will really make things easier in the long run. An easy way to handle this from the very start of your new business is to open a checking account in your business' name. Deposit all receipts from your business, cash and checks, into this account. Pay all expenses out of this account, making a record of the payment. If you are audited, Rule #1 can save your life! And even if you are not, Rule #1 can save your business.

Whether you opt for a sole proprietorship (you are the only owner), a partnership (two or more share the business), a LLC (limited liability company), or incorporation (the business becomes a separate entity, with you as an employee and stockholder), you will be wise if you seek the help of a knowledgeable and honest accountant. As you grow, possibly a lawyer specializing in business law will be worth the cost.

Setting Up

Computers and their application are discussed in the next chapter. You will probably end up keeping your records on a computer, so it is best to start doing so now, if at all possible. Shop carefully for a software package that will meet your needs and expand with your business.

Some of you, however, may opt to start out with basic ledgers. Companies like Dome have been putting out simplified bookkeeping and payroll accounting books for many years. These can be found in office supply and discount stores. In such a book, you can find the ledgers for receipts, materials, and other expenses, as well as payroll for a small operation (ten or less people). These books constitute a simplified do-it-yourself accounting kit.

Whatever system you decide upon, understanding the basics will help you keep straight in your mind how your money sifts through the system and why, unfortunately, you seem to end up keeping less of it than you thought.

So you decided on a name for your business, say Acme Service. You went to the bank and opened a checking account in the business name. You got your first job — a one-time job cleaning a carpet or painting a garage, but it's a start. Whether you are paid in cash or with a check, start now with the self-discipline of (1) marking down the payment on your accounts receivable ledger and (2) resisting the temptation to spend any of the money for personal use. (See Figure 9.1 for a sample of an accounts receivable ledger.)

Next you find what you have been looking for, a regular contract customer, the ABC Company. They want your service on a regular basis — weekly, monthly,

FIGURE 9.1: Sample Accounts Receivable Ledger

Receipts for month of: October 2000			
Date	Received From	Amount	Check No./ Cash
Oct 4	M. Johnson (carpet cleaning)	$175.00	Cash
Oct 7	Al's Café (window cleaning)	75.00	1520
Oct 11	Star Jewelry (window cleaning)	70.00	2496
Oct 11	ABC Company (office cleaning)	1,500.00	11849
Oct 18	Ace Realty (rental house cleanup)	425.00	8507
Oct 21	Al's Café (window cleaning)	75.00	1535
Oct 25	Star Jewelry (window cleaning)	70.00	2511
Month's Total		$2,390.00	
Year to Date		$21,278.00	

or more — and you agree on a price to be billed at the end of the month. To keep track of the work you have done and what the company has and has not paid for, you could set up a ledger for this customer. (See Figure 9.2 for a sample contract customer ledger.)

In the meantime you have spent money. You rented equipment to do the job, you bought a piece of equipment, supplies, or gas to take you to the jobs. All these expenses are paid through your company checking account and recorded on an expense ledger. (See Figure 9.3.) The gas can be paid for with a gas credit card or through a petty cash fund you set up. Remember to have receipts to cover all petty cash withdrawals. Even if you pay cash for gas, always ask for a cash receipt.

At the end of the month (or week, if you like) you can total your expenses and receipts on an accounting sheet (see Figure 9.4). This form tallies all totals from all other ledgers and gives you that important *bottom-line total*. The way this

FIGURE 9.2: Sample Contract Customer Ledger

ABC Company   555-7777
1212 First Street   Contact: Mr. Robert Jones
Mytown, SC 2000

Description of Work	Date Billed	Amount Billed	Date Paid	Amount Paid	Check Number
(Start work August 15)					
August—Wks of 8/14, 21,28	8/31/00	$900.00	9/12/00	$900.00	11685
Carpet Cleaning 8/18/00	8/31/00	$385.00	9/12/00	$385.00	11685
Sept.—Wkes of 9/5, 12,19,26	9/30/00	$1,500.00	10/10/00	$1,500.00	11849
Oct—Wks of 10/2,9,16,23	10/30/00	$1,500.00			
Total Receipts for Year:					

FIGURE 9.3: Sample Expense Ledger

Receipts for month of: October 2000

Date	Paid Out To	Amount	Check Number	Account Number
Oct.3	E-Z Rental (carpet machine)	$40.00	185	15
Oct.5	*The Times* (newspaper ad)	$35.00	186	2
Oct.11	Ace Janitorial Supply	$185.75	187	8
Oct.11	One Stop Gas (for work van)	$18.75	188	3
Oct.14	Postage	$36.00	189	11
Oct.19	Fix-It Shop (repair vacuum)	$20.00	190	16
Total		$335.00		

FIGURE 9.4: Sample Monthly Accounting Sheet

Monthly accounting for month of: October 2000

Account Number	Category	This Month	Year to Date	Total
1.	Accounting		$375.00	$375.00
2.	Advertising	$35.00	$90.00	$126.00
3.	Auto Expense	$18.75	$205.85	$224.60
4.	Insurance — employee			
5.	Insurance — liability, workers' compensation		$150.00	$150.00
6.	Insurance — other		$200.00	$200.00
7.	Equipment		$1,739.56	$1,739.56
8.	Supplies	$185.75	$1,279.35	$1,465.10
9.	Legal		$75.00	$75.00
10.	Miscellaneous		$85.50	$85.50
11.	Office Expense	$36.00	$187.20	$223.20
12.	Payroll			
13.	Payroll — FICA			
14.	Payroll — U.I.			
15.	Rent	$40.00	$195.54	$235.54
16.	Repairs	$20.00	$45.00	$65.00
17.	Taxes		$334.50	$334.50
18.	Utilities			
19.				
20.				
	Total	$335.50	$4,962.50	$5,299.00
	Accounts Receivable	$2,390.00	$21,278.00	$23,668.00
	Net (account receivable less total)	$2,053.50	$16,315.50	$18,369.00

works is when you get to the bottom of the form, you subtract your total expenses from your accounts receivable. Then you will have your first idea of how you are doing and if you can give yourself a paycheck. Don't be upset if you are in the "red" in the beginning. Keep doing quality work and that will all change.

Any system or computer program should give you the same results, though they may go about it in different ways. If you can understand this simple layout, it should help you when you are trying to sort out your books.

All this may seem complicated and tedious at first, but you will get used to keeping track of it soon. The value of using a system like this is that your monthly accounting sheet will show you how much money you have made, how much you have spent, and where your money is going. The best part of all this is, if you keep this record up to date all year, you need only take your last month's page to your accountant. That page should provide your accountant with almost everything needed to prepare your business tax return — no shuffling through shoe boxes for lost receipts. Be sure to keep those receipts together for each tax year in case you are audited. Put them all in a large clearly-marked envelope, and you will come out of any audit successfully.

There are a number of quality accounting systems on the market, some in book form, some for use with a computer. (See next chapter.) To illustrate how this works we have used a simple computer spreadsheet to compile the samples, in this book. If you are computer literate the spreadsheet program will keep track of all your transactions and total them up for you as well.

Taxes

Now that you are self-employed, no one is taking out income tax and FICA or social security for you. Here is where many businesses get in trouble. As you write checks to yourself from the business profits, remember — even when starting out at the lowest income levels, a safe rule of thumb would be to put away 25 to 35 cents of each dollar you make. Self-employed people generally pay their taxes quarterly (due April 15, June 15, September 15, and January 15 of the following year), and your accountant can help you get set up for this.

Because it is a quarterly payment it, is so tempting to use that money for other things, but that trap could cost you your business and get you in trouble with the Internal Revenue Service. So put that money in an inaccessible place. One small businessman opened a savings account. He deposited 25 cents for every dollar he took in and earned interest, too. He always had his quarterly deposit when it was due.

Note: Because you are the owner of your business, your taxable income will be based on what your business made, not how much you drew out for your use. Once again, the net total on your monthly accounting sheet will give you an idea where you are. It won't be exact because some equipment is depreciated over a period of years, even though you paid for it this year. (Leave that headache to your accountant.) But you still want to keep an eye on that bottom line.

Payroll

Suppose you land that nice contract you have been working on. Now you are going to need help. You started with family, but they still expect to be paid. You will need to set up a payroll system, but you might check with your accountant again. The tax laws give some leeway when your employees are family.

However, if you are working hard to build your business, it won't be long before you hire outside help. (See the chapter on Personnel for guidelines.)

At this point, if you are not inclined to recordkeeping, you might look to a trusted, qualified family member, friend, or employee to look after the payroll. Another option: your accountant may offer a service or could recommend one.

Don't let these details scare you. It's really not that bad. It will take more of that discipline we discussed in managing the business money. You will be withholding tax money and in some cases matching the amounts (i.e., FICA). Particularly when you are just starting out with a few employees, some of this money will not be due until the end or the month, quarter, or even the year. It may be in your bank account, but . . . .

Rule 2
Withheld tax money is not your money — don't touch it.

Think of yourself as a banker entrusted with other people's money. If need be, set up a separate account and put it there—maybe one that earns interest. That's what bankers do.

You may wish to purchase a payroll program for your computer or a book from your office supply store. It has all the forms and lays out your deductions and procedures fairly simply for you. Your accountant can help you obtain the tax table books you will need for figuring the federal, state, and local withholding for your employees. When you do your payroll, check your figures closely before typing the paychecks. Errors are easy to make and sometimes hard to find.

Keeping books will serve you for up to a dozen or so employees. Beyond that, or from the beginning, you will definitely want to look into a computer payroll program. They are so easy once they are set up. You punch in the hours for each employee and it prints out the checks and tells you how much tax needs to be withheld. Usually the programs will even prepare the quarterly payroll tax statement and print up the W-2s at the end of the year.

In conclusion, don't let the bookkeeping aspect of running a business get you down. Once you discipline yourself to keep everything in order, you will enjoy being able to put your finger on where you are financially at any given moment or having the funds put aside when a large tax deposit is due. That can help you tremendously when contemplating a larger purchase, and it avoids the year-end hassle to get everything together.

10

Computers and Your Business

"To err is human .... But, to really foul things up takes a computer."

——Anonymous

In this age of technology, the Internet, and voice mail, most people have or will have a computer. When it comes to running a business, it is becoming a necessity. Therefore, it is appropriate we explore ways to use this marvelous tool in your business.

You may feel that your budget absolutely prohibits your starting out with a computer. But have you read the ads lately? Prices for them have come down so much recently, and they are a legitimate business expense if used for such.

Because computer technology is so much a part of our lives, you will find it the very core of your record keeping, billing, and communication. Like it or not, it will only become more so as time goes on. Therefore, it would be best to start out setting up your system on the computer. That will save you from having to redo everything later on.

You can keep some of your financial and payroll records on a simple spreadsheet. Most computer systems have a spreadsheet program. With a little practice, it can serve you well. A word processor can put out crisp, neat letters and even create a letterhead for you. It will also check your spelling and grammar before you print it out. What a long way we have come from the days of the manual typewriter, carbon copies, and smudged erasures.

If you will be running a payroll system, keeping track of customers, billing, or assigning employee jobs, there are many programs available at a reasonable cost — less than $200. As you know, technology and available programs are becoming more and more advanced and (best of all) user-friendly. Every industry today has its own variety of programs, and service businesses are no exception.

> *You must understand that your computer has it in for you. The proof is that it makes you think it really does what you tell it to do.*
>
> — Anonymous

tion. There are specific programs to keep your books, do your payroll, estimate jobs and help you prepare a bid. Programs specifically designed for service businesses with many small jobs can help you keep track of every facet of your business. Some of these programs will be discussed in this chapter, and information as to how to obtain them is in the Appendix.

Some programs will run within the Windows platform, but do not provide the capability of having multiple windows available at the same time. Many advertise that they will integrate with your word processor, and that can save a lot of time. What you might be looking for would be an integrated program to show:

- all sales and credits
- all payments and debits
- all open transactions (unpaid invoices)
- all closed transactions (paid invoices)
- accounts receivable report
- payroll reports
- income statement
- balance sheet
- task scheduling
- job costing and pricing

Your goal is to save time and money by having the computer do the jobs that are routine. (For example, computers can put out a mass mailing in a fraction of the time it used to take.) However, for a little more, there are programs to help you with more difficult tasks. Some include a program for job bidding and estimating. This can be really helpful if you are as yet unsure of yourself in this area, or if you have a large, complex bid to prepare. Whether tracking a job, your customers, your employees, or accounting information, many work as a database, reducing the need to keep upgrading many varied files. Once all your information is loaded, one of these fully-integrated systems can locate any information you need in seconds.

Rimrock Technologies, listed in the Appendix, has taken the many tasks involved in running your business and put together a package consisting of a number of modules that can be purchased separately or together. They work together well, and you have the option of buying only what you feel you will use.

The widely-advertised QuickBooks and QuickBooks Pro may fill your needs nicely. They offer payroll, accounting, estimating, and time tracking and work well with Microsoft Word or Excel. A phone call can get you a free demonstration version to test before buying.

Check out the software stores for things that may help you. Some packages help with legal documents for your corporation. Some will prepare and print checks and invoices, electronic index card systems, help with employee evaluations, and remind you of your upcoming tax deadlines—even your wedding anniversary. Buy the ones that can be of genuine help, and don't waste your time or money on the ones that you can do without.

The Down Side and a Solution

There are a few negative aspects of all this sophisticated programming. Payroll programs are usually sold separately. Most systems require considerable time to set up and enter all the data. When you are just staring out in business, you need to be spending most of your time out in the field getting new business. A solution might be to have a computer-literate family member or a friend do this set-up work.

In my research for this book, I looked at a number of programs specifically for service businesses. You will find, as in the case of all customized software, that they can be a bit pricey. For a complete package (including work orders, schedules, bidding information, and inventory), $1,700 to $5,000 is not unusual.

However, one software company that evolved from an experienced service company is offering an exceptional package of five software programs for under $1,000. In fact, if you only want one of the programs, they will sell it to you for $250. (For example, you may want just their bidding program.) I have used them, and it is clear that they are experienced contract cleaners. Their five programs can be adapted to most of the service businesses in this book. They are listed first in the Appendix under computer programs.

One thing you must remember, however: No one program can help you unless you feed it the right information. For example, with the bidding program, you still need to know the magic formula for pricing. But don't panic, it's in this book.

As you organize your business, you must allow for the human element. You may set up this elaborate program and have a crew scheduled to be one place at 9 AM and to be somewhere else at 11 AM, only to find they were delayed by a problem at the 9 AM appointment, got stuck in traffic, got lost, or detoured to a fast-food restaurant for a coffee break. So the scheduling should not be too rigid.

Organize your work into files and directories that work for you, keeping related files together. Frequently, perhaps daily, back up all your work. That is, make a copy of what you have done on a separate diskette to protect your work should the computer fail. If you have quite a bit to save, a zip drive is easy to add to your computer, and it will save large amounts of data.

Crash Course for the Computer Novice

Think of your computer as a filing cabinet. Disk drives in your computer are like the various drawers in the filing cabinet. The folders are like the file folders in the drawer. Each folder can hold a number of files, much as a number of papers can go into each file folder. The computer will ask you to name these files as they are saved. Choose a name that will identify the contents for you for easy reference.

Of course, your computer will need a printer. Some come with printers as part of the package. A copy machine is also a wise investment for any small office.

The Internet

Having your own Web page is becoming popular with many businesses, large and small. Whether you choose to advertise in this manner depends on your market. Most service businesses just starting out will not lend themselves to this. But don't close your mind to the potential of this powerful tool. The time may come when most business is done on the Internet.

Perhaps you can find suppliers who will provide what you need at a better price than you can get locally. You could make contacts with others in similar service businesses, which may be helpful.

Since almost everyone has e-mail these days, you can save time and postage by sending your message this way. Documents could also be faxed through your computer to anywhere in the world in a fraction of the time it would take using any delivery service.

The Scary Part

That state-of-the-art computer and software package you bought last month is already on its way to becoming obsolete! In three years or so you may be forced to replace it with the newest model that will also be obsolete in no time. That is why shopping for a quality software package that will adapt or easily be upgraded is essential to your sanity and budget.

Other Technology

While we are on the subject, there are other gadgets that are fast becoming indispensable in business today.

So many businesses now have fax machines that you may find investing in one an early necessity. Look at it this way: You've got a bid deadline and it has to be submitted tonight across town. A fax machine could save that trip and give you more time.

Computers are going miniature. Palm computer units can go out to the job estimate site with you. You can enter the specifications in it and then plug it into your main unit when you get back to the office. Can't wait that long? Some will e-mail the information back for you.

Oh, yes, everyone seems to have a cell or digital phone in their pocket now. Cell phones are even being sold in convenience stores! With the price of this technology coming down, you probably will find it a useful tool. You can even add features such as voice mail to ensure you don't miss an important call. Word of caution: These phones can quickly become expensive if abused. The best way to use them is to choose a reasonable package and then stay within the package time you have. Besides that, if you drive and use a wireless phone, your driving performance equals that of a legally drunk driver.

After all this talk about computers, there is one more important statement: Computers are not for everyone! If you find you are running a one-person or very small operation and don't even know how to turn a computer on, you can still run a fine business using good, old-fashioned paper. People have been doing that for years.

Whatever you decide, it looks like computers and their related technology are here to stay. Computers, copiers, fax machines, cell phones, and Web pages — they are all new tools to help you with your business. Use them wisely and they will serve you well. But don't let their use and cost eat up all your time and resources — that is not why you are in business.

Complaints

"The wheel that squeaks the loudest is the one that gets the grease."

— Josh Billings

The way a person in business handles complaints can greatly determine success or failure. Therefore, this is a very serious issue, and if you operate a service business, you should be aware of this.

Unfortunately, when hearing a complaint many ignore it (maybe due to pride), attempt to justify it before looking into the facts, or assume that it couldn't be their fault. The feeling is that the customer or some of the customer's employees must be having a bad day. "It couldn't be me or my people at fault!"

Another source of complaints as a small business grows is the employees. They often come in with complaints and the way you deal with them will ultimately affect your business. How? Disgruntled employees do poor work as a rule. Thus morale becomes low and this spreads like wildfire among the workers. On the other hand, workers who feel they are heard by their boss will perform better, show greater loyalty, and be more industrious. You may not respond to every complaint in the way that employees anticipated, but the fact that you listened will go a long way.

How to View Complaints

How then should we view a complaint? Have you ever watched a movie about a bomb that was planted in a building and the police sent the bomb squad in to diffuse it? Well, liken the complaint to a bomb threat and you (if you are responsive) are the bomb squad. Just like the literal bomb squad, take each and every complaint seriously. Because if you don't diffuse them, they will explode into customer or employee discontent and result in loss of business or a growing morale problem.

At the very least, ignored complaints will start the customer looking much closer at your work. Some customers even begin to play games with you, such as hiding a piece of paper behind or under something you are supposed to clean and counting the days it takes you to find it. The customer also may begin to nitpick and make time-consuming demands. One way or another, you are headed for trouble.

An experienced businessperson knows that, no matter how good your service is, there always will be complaints. No one is perfect, and even the best will slip up sometime. But there is no excuse for ignored complaints.

Typical Complaints

Some complaints deal with performance. The following are some typical complaints you might have to diffuse or deal with.

Performance: *"You didn't dust my desk last night!"*

"The bathroom wasn't clean!"

(For regular service cleaning-type businesses, dusting and bathrooms are the number one complaint in a national poll.)

"The carpet you cleaned still has spots."

"The paint is not the color I wanted."

"The grass looks burned."

Then there is the complaint we definitely do not want to get — the accusation of theft.

Theft: *"Some of my tools are missing from the shelf!"*

"The box of important papers I put next to the trash can is gone!"

How Do You Diffuse a Complaint?

How should you handle a complaint? Immediately, if not sooner. That's the key. Remember that complaints are like crabgrass in your lawn. You must respond quickly or the problem will get out of hand. Complaints, whether true or untrue, can eventually make you look bad. The complainer is mainly interested in your response time to a complaint. If you are quick, you will probably retain that account or customer. (Some successful services promise a response within 60 minutes.)

If you are providing your service for another business, often an employee of your customer will make the complaint. When responding to a complaint, whether you use the phone or go in person (most effective), contact and talk to the person who made the complaint — with the customer's permission, of course. Listen carefully. Don't argue and don't be defensive. Be reasonable and intensely interested in what they have to say. Promise you will correct the problem immediately — and do it.

Sometimes the simple act of verbalizing the complaint will help the person see it really is something petty (let them come to that conclusion themselves), but he or she appreciates that you are taking the time to listen and act, if necessary. It could be a small thing has been overlooked and can be easily fixed.

One very important point to remember, while you are diffusing, is that it is important to ask questions. The answers may reveal the real source of the complaint and help you find a resolution.

You might try asking pointed, yet non-incriminating, questions.

- *"When did you first notice this problem ... ? "*

- *"Was the problem with any particular fixture in the bathroom, or was it overall ... ? "*

- *"Why do you feel your grass has that burned look? Could it be the weather?"*

In some cases, the person may be looking for something not scheduled in your work contract. Tactfully point that out and explain when it will be done. Some examples of this are as follows:

- On an office-cleaning contract, the customer may be looking for high dusting to have been done on a Monday night and the contract schedules it to be done on a Friday night.

- After a cleaning, carpeting often wicks up soil from deep in the pile. You may need to go back and get those places.

- Paint sometimes doesn't dry exactly as the paint chip indicates, for a number of reasons. Letting the customer know this fact ahead of time can prepare him or her for that.

- Often grass is burned in the summer when the customer requires you to set your mowers too close to the ground, hoping to save on the overall times it needs to be mowed. Or it could be you are cutting it the wrong time of day and you may need to work out a time with the customer that is better for the grass.

Theft

In complaints about theft, experience shows that when working on the premises of another business, it is the customer's own employees who are guilty. Statistics show that employee theft is a leading cause of losses in the workplace. They have greater opportunity and often feel it is owed them because they aren't paid what they are worth.

It is all too convenient to blame an outsider. If you and your crew are faceless people who come in after everyone has left, it is human nature to view you with suspicion. In most cases, if the customer's employees knew you or your employees better, it would eliminate a lot of these complaints.

Here is an idea that has worked well for some. Why not ask the facility manager if you could send in a few of your key employees two or three hours early during regular business hours to begin some preliminary work? They, of course, wouldn't run any noisy equipment or get in the way of their customers. When your people are visible, clients see the same smiling faces each day you work on that job, and trust grows. This also works in nicely with an energy saving program. If working inside a large facility during regular hours, lights, heat, or air conditioning will run less and thus save money. Of course, this suggestion will only work for a very limited number of service businesses. But it is extremely effective when applied.

Once again, asking sincere, non-incriminating questions might help the complainer realize that the item in question was not taken, but moved. Or in the case of the papers left in a box on top of the trash can, perhaps they were mistaken for trash.

These same principles apply when you work in a private home. Establishing trust early on will cut down on complaints. If you move something to perform some task, be sure to replace it, or get the homeowner's permission to move it somewhere else.

As discussed in an earlier chapter, your image goes a long way towards how people view you and your company. That is why it is so important that you and your people look clean-cut and trustworthy. If you do, you may find theft complaints will not be such a problem.

The Complaint Sheet

If your service takes you to the same office or business on a daily, weekly, or monthly basis, you can also diffuse a lot of complaints (and prevent them from climbing the corporate ladder) with a simple piece of paper, a complaint sheet.

On the top of the complaint sheet you might employ a bit of comic relief — another way to diffuse complaints. The cartoon of a man crying sends the subtle message that you are aware of the upset we all feel at times and will deal with their complaint with empathy. Perhaps an appropriate cartoon or comic character will suit your situation. (See Figure 11.1.)

With the facility manager's permission, attach the sheet to the outside of the door of the supply or janitor's closets or on their company bulletin board. When appropriate you might even hang a copy of your work schedule next to it so that the employee with the complaint can see what is supposed to be done and when.

Require your employees on that job to check it first thing every time they come to work. They will want to correct the matter at that time if it is in accordance with your contract or agreement. Be sure they note on the slip when it was corrected, then replace with a clean sheet soon afterward. If you are not personally on that particular job every day, be sure you also check it when you are making your PR calls. Even if there is nothing written on it for a year, never stop checking it. Bombs usually go off when we least expect them to.

FIGURE 11.1: Complaint Sheet

Acme Service

List below any complaint about our work

Complaint	Area	Date

Selling Yourself

"A man without a smiling face must not open a shop."

— Chinese Proverb

You are almost there. Following the guidelines covered so far, you have probably considered your abilities and interests, and the types of businesses that you feel would succeed for you. You have put together a business plan that is realistic and workable. Perhaps you even have gotten your feet wet with a few small jobs. But have you considered your greatest sales tool?

You and Your Business

Your service business may be the best in your area, but the customer will be looking at you. In the chapter covering how to get the business, there was a lot of emphasis on personal appearance and first impressions. You will never be able to show how good you really are if you can't get a chance to show your customer what you can do.

How do you get that first chance to show them your stuff? Sometimes that is a challenge. But remember, you are selling yourself first and foremost. Start at the very basic level with a total personal self-evaluation.

Perhaps that sounds drastic. Well, it could be, or maybe not. Get up and look at yourself in a mirror, preferably a full-length mirror. Before you start thinking how good looking you are, pretend you are looking at a total stranger.

Put on your uniform or business suit, whatever you will be wearing when you first meet potential customers. Honestly, what do you see? Look closely at your dress and grooming. You may enjoy a style that is in fashion, but there is a standard in business. Classic-cut clothing and neat clean-cut grooming is the standard that instills confidence in business. Look at television ads illustrating people in business. You may see a commercial for a uniform service business, such as pest control. The person in the commercial is shown in a clean, neat uniform with a neat haircut — the kind of person you wouldn't mind letting in your home or office. A man in a business requiring a business suit is also shown with a clean, pressed suit, neat shirt, and matching tie, all nicely coordinated, without wild patterns. His shoes are shined. This is called power dressing for success. You would trust that person with the keys to your house or office building.

Women in business, too, need to power dress for success. Cheap-looking, ill-fitting, too tight, or provocative clothing will convey the wrong message. This has no place in business. You want to be considered a professional, so you should look professional.

- Total personal self-evaluation
- Power dress for success
- Neat sales materials
- Practice sessions

Are you into the casual, comfortable look when you are at home? Well, leave those clothes at home and get yourself some suitable clothes for your service business. That means a neat uniform-type outfit or smock or a classic-cut business suit. Then when you look at yourself in the mirror, you will look like someone who is serious about business.

Once again, the business world has a standard, and this is expected of men and women. Success or failure often results from the image projected.

Your Materials

Now you look sharp. Next you want to look at the sales material you will be carrying. Maybe you will need an attaché case or a folder with an order book inside. Whatever the case, look closely at what you plan to use. If it is in bad shape or bad taste (gaudy color or emblems), go shopping for a new one. Classic leather in black or brown is always a good choice. Remember you are power dressing — strictly class all the way. Have your materials neatly organized and try to anticipate what you will need. You may never have made a sales call before, but you don't want your potential client to know that.

By the way, before you leave in your car or work truck, how long has it been since it was washed?

Practice Sessions

As you put together your sales presentation, have a practice session at home. Do it in front of a mirror and/or with a family member playing the part of the prospect. First of all, practice greeting and shaking hands. Shaking hands? Yes, many people in business read a lot into a good, firm handshake. Don't break any bones, but don't act like you are afraid to touch either. Some people nervously pump the hand of the other person or forget to let go after two or three shakes. This may sound simplistic, but this is, after all, your first impression.

As you speak, be mindful of "word whiskers." These are the "ahs" and "ums" you might feel compelled to put in the middle of your sentences. They are very distracting and give the impression you are not sure of yourself. Look the person in the eye. Your aim is to project a positive attitude, but not arrogant or overbearing.

All this may seem like a lot to remember, but with practice it will become natural to you. If you hope to get and keep good customers, you will need to keep your professional image going. On your frequent — and they should be frequent — PR calls, always treat the customer professionally and look your best.

Attitude

Customer retention is a real problem for most service businesses. Blame is often put on the customer, but think about the times you have called someone, like a plumber. How many did you have to call to get one to agree to come when you wanted, do the work right the first time, and not overcharge you? If you found such a service, you would not call anyone else the next time you needed a plumber. In fact, you would tell all your friends to call this plumber.

Your customer expects you to be available when contracting you for work. Provide the service at a fair price and you will keep that customer.

Now that you have begun to establish yourself in your service business, you may be thinking of other related services you could add to increase profits.

Diversify or Specialize

"It does not take much strength to do things,
but it requires great strength to decide on what to do."

— Elbert Hubbard

You probably have already given considerable thought to the type of business you want to operate. That's your dream — the perfect situation. Great! However, the difference between success and failure in most business undertakings is the right approach for your circumstances and market. The basic guidelines presented here should prove helpful.

If, on the other hand, you are not sure what you want to do or how to go about achieving your goal, a number of the more successful service businesses are covered in the remaining chapters. There are hundreds of different possibilities. Selected here are about 30 with good overall potential. Perhaps one of them is your chosen service business. A number of compatible services will be listed. Even if your service business is something not covered here, some of the add-ons may give you an idea of diversity potential for your business.

One thing to consider is that most service businesses have slow and busy seasons. However, the beauty of the service industry is that it is very easy to diversify into a related field. This serves the two-fold purpose of keeping you and your people busy during the slow times and adding services for existing customers that increase your profit margin.

Each business opportunity covers the type of customer for your service, what is involved, how to price your work, what insurance, equipment and supplies you will need, and how or if a sales manual will help. Finally, ideas for profitable add-on services are discussed, as well as tips or often-overlooked things that can help you succeed.

Service businesses covered in this book are:

- Apartment preparation service
- Automobile detailing
- Carpet cleaning
- Ceiling cleaning and wall washing
- Chimney cleaning
- Computer and office machine cleaning
- Concrete cleaning and sealing
- Graffiti cleaning
- Home allergy proofing
- Floor maintenance
- Landscaping service
- Lighting service
- Maid service
- New construction cleanup
- Office cleaning
- Painting
- Parking lot cleaning
- Pest control service
- Pressure washing
- Restaurant cleaning
- Restroom service
- Security guard service
- Smoke and fire restoration

- Stone cleaning (marble)
- Swimming pool service
- Temporary help service
- Trash removal
- Tree trimming
- Water damage restoration
- Window cleaning
- Yacht cleaning

As your eyes ran down the above list, no doubt a number of the listings are promising possibilities, perhaps things you hadn't thought of doing. In the service industry there are endless possibilities available to make a good living. What works for you will be determined by many factors. Some of these are your personal desire, your ability to organize and manage, and the needs in your locality.

If your ability to organize is somewhat limited, then you would be wise to limit yourself to one or two special services and keep the size of your company modest. If, on the other hand, you have talent in this area, your opportunities to expand are unlimited.

Another aspect is the needs of your locality. If your local phone book is loaded with listings for carpet cleaners, perhaps another field will get the results you want — and you can offer carpet cleaning on the side. Or you may live where it snows eight or more months a year. You probably won't be able to support yourself with a swimming pool service — unless there are a lot of indoor pools or ski resorts with super-heated pools nearby. So the point is to take a realistic look at your market potential, but don't be too quick to conclude a certain service will not succeed in your area. Using other fields as a backup, try sticking your toe in the water. You may discover an untapped market.

Additional Reading

This book will help you start and successfully run a service business. The techniques work. So do you need more information? Yes, and you always will. Never stop reading and learning. It can be the difference between success and failure. I have an extensive business book library that I have built up over the years and I continue to add to it. In there I still discover useful ideas.

If you wish to expand your knowledge, you may wish to look into some of the books listed below. They are in my personal library and some are used as textbooks in classes I teach.

SmartStart Your [state] *Business* — by the Editorial Staff at Oasis Press.

Business Owner's Guide to Accounting & Bookkeeping — Jose Placencia, Bruce Welge and Don Oliver, published by Oasis Press.

A Company Policy & Personnel Handbook — Ardella Ramey and Carl R.J. Sniffen, published by Oasis Press.

Power Marketing for Small Business — Jody Horner, published by Oasis Press.

Smile Training Isn't Enough — Richard S. Gallagher, published by Oasis Press.

Section II

Now that you have the basics, perhaps you would like to see how these principles can be applied to a specific service business that you feel would suit you and your talents most.

The remaining chapters each cover a different service business. Each tells you about who will use your service, what is involved, your needs (insurance, sales manual, equipment and supplies), pricing, and add-ons to increase your profits. The final tips cover little details many often have to learn through trial and error.

Perhaps you are already acquainted with the basics, possibly having established a service business. You can still find these remaining chapters a valuable tool. How? You could expand into related specialties, and within these chapters are the pricing and marketing information that will get your foot in the door.

CHAPTER
14

Apartment Preparation Service

In the United States people have moved into over eight million apartments in one year. Apartment dwellers, on the average, will move once every three years. There is probably a total of more than 22 million apartments. Traditionally, the cleaning and preparation for a new tenant has been done in-house, or the departing tenant is supposed to do it and does a minimum get-your-deposit-back job. This is changing to outside services in a number of areas.

What Is Involved

You will provide a basic maid service. In some ways it will be easier without the tenants present and the clutter of their personal belongings. However, although you will have fewer things to clean, what will be left will be dirtier than normal. Spots, dents, scratches, or holes in the wall from pictures will need your attention as they really show up in an empty room.

An enterprising service will also provide some profitable options for the apartment owner — painting, carpet cleaning, and some fix-it work. The key is speed. The owner wants the apartment ready as soon as possible. Provide fast, responsive service and you will do very well in this specialty.

Most in this business have found that advertising gets them started, but word of mouth from established landlord customers brings in most of the business.

Sales Manual

A simple sales manual includes references and much of the information that you would include for a maid service. Be sure to develop a separate, comprehensive price list as well.

Insurance

Liability and bonding will no doubt be all you need to start. Happily, it should not be very expensive as you get started. As you take on employees, you will need to add such things as unemployment insurance, and workers' compensation.

Equipment and Supplies

Your needs here are much the same as you would use for maid, painting, and carpet cleaning services, plus some general household tools for fixing a leaking toilet, water faucet, or light fixture. In addition, you may need to replace a door or window.

Put together a good toolbox with basic tools. You can start out with tools from home and replace them with tools purchased for your business as you can afford it.

As to cleaning supplies, purchase a good carryall and stock it with some basic supplies.

- Cleanser
- Chlorine bleach
- Wall cleaner
- Carpet spot remover
- Disinfectant cleaner
- Stainless steel cleaner
- Wood paneling cleaner and scratch cover up

- A supply of paper towels and cloth rags
- Scrub brushes and rubber gloves

Next you want to be sure you have:

- Mops, brooms, etc.
- A good vacuum (preferably an upright with a hose attachment)
- A wet/shop vacuum
- A carpet cleaning machine (can be rented and later purchased)

As you can see, most of these things are common household cleaning items you probably already have. As your budget allows, build your business inventory of supplies and equipment.

Pricing

You can easily charge $80 to $220 per apartment or 8 to 10 cents per square foot. Of course, large, luxurious oceanfront, lakefront, or penthouse apartments can at least double those figures. For painting pricing, see the section on Painting. For pricing carpet cleaning, please refer to that section.

On fix-up work you can charge anywhere from $35 to $50 per hour.

Profitable Add-Ons

This can combine nicely with a construction clean-up, maid service, or painting service. It can also stand on its own in some areas of the country.

Final Tips

The customers will give you some tough jobs to test you out in the beginning. Take it on the chin and do your best. It will pay off. Once you establish the fact you can be depended on for quality work and honest pricing, the work will pour in.

Cities, college towns, and resort and coastal areas are very good markets for this specialty. But don't overlook any tourist locations with high volumes of apartments. A good and well-organized team of cleaners (say, four) can do up to ten units a day.

Automobile Detailing

This is a business in which you probably began to develop skills when you got your first car. If you are like most of us, it wasn't a new one. It needed a lot of cleaning up. So you polished and scrubbed to bring out the shine and make it look as sharp as possible when you pulled into your school's parking lot.

Who Will Use My Service

- Car dealers
- Individual car owners

What Is Involved

Car detailing is little more than what you did with your first car. Now you find yourself calling on your local car dealers and offering to do the same thing to all their used cars. Your market can also include the private car owner who has either seen your advertising or passed by your garage (if you have one).

This is an excellent one- or two-man operation. An enterprising student can even effectively do it after school. A full-time worker needing to moonlight for extra money can take it on as a part-time job. However, don't underestimate the potential here. An organized full-time, one-man operation can earn from $30,000 to $50,000 per year. Here is another big plus. You can enter this business on a shoestring. Perhaps a few hundred up to a few thousand dollars will be all you would need.

Sales Manual

Your primary and regular customers will be automobile dealerships. You will want to show before-and-after pictures. List references. Since this work rarely involves a contract, the sample contract shown earlier won't be necessary.

Insurance

You'll need liability and bonding, and employee-related insurances if you hire help.

Equipment and Supplies

Some things you will need are as follows:

- *Power buffer*. First you may want a heavy-duty power buffer, but caution is needed. Be careful as you develop your skill with these buffers. They can burn the paint off a car, and that can be expensive.

- *Orbital buffer*. This is easier to use and more useful than a power buffer. It doesn't have the power of the regular buffer to remove heavy oxidation. However, it is a safer buffer to start out with.

- *Wet/dry vacuum*. A plastic one to start with is fine. Wait until you are established to buy the heavy-duty stainless steel model.

- *Pressure washer*. For vehicles, 1,500 to 2,000 psi is nice. Refer to the chapter on the pressure washing business.

- *Waxes and cleaners*. Do not buy the cheapest. There are some new high tech car waxes and interior cleaners on the market today that do an amazing job. They can substantially reduce your labor time per job. These are worth the difference in cost.

- *Interior cleaners.* A good carpet cleaner and spot remover; glass cleaner; leather and plastic cleaner; solvent gum remover; and finally, an assortment of soft rags and paper towels.

- *Assortment of brushes.* There are a number of soft to firm bristle brushes of various shapes perfect for cleaning in crevices of the interior, particularly the dash. Specialty stores have them, but look first in discount stores and you may find what you need to get started on a budget. A toothbrush will often do the job.

Pricing

A full hand wash may go for $15 to $25 or more. A full detail may go for $70 to $100 or more. The full detail job will generally include:

- washing and waxing (clean trunk and door jams).
- cleaning tires.
- polishing wheel rims and chrome.
- vacuuming and cleaning seats and upholstery.
- applying a silicone-type product to all vinyl, including dash (after you cleaned out all the crevices with a brush).
- new car smell. (The chemical scent adds that perfect finishing touch.)

Be sure to make it clear in your pricing that cars involving extra work will cost more.

As with all service businesses, you will want to work on production time. Two experienced men should be able to detail a car in two hours or less. One man could take up to four hours.

Also, as you develop your price list, time each function of detailing separately. Then, using a rate of $25 to $35 per hour, you should be able to price it out. Because of the volume, you can afford to offer car dealers a better rate than the person who only comes in once or has one car to detail.

As your operation grows and you hire helpers, you should be realizing at least a 25 percent profit margin after you have paid all salaries and expenses. If you are not, your pricing is too low or someone is laying down on the job.

Profitable Add-Ons

Optional services to boost your profit include:

- rust preventative.

- windshield glass repair.

- engine painting.

- use of "high tech" long-lasting silicone glazes.

- upholstery and vinyl tear repair.

- head liner repair or replacement.

- treating upholstered seats with protective treatment or some type of waterproofing after cleaning.

- offering mobile wash/wax service — where you come to the home or business of the customer.

Each add-on mentioned requires products that have a wide range in cost. Careful shopping can keep your costs down, but don't buy the cheapest unless you have tried it and know it will do the job. Your supplier often is aware of what is being charged in your area and often will help you.

Another profitable add-on might be pressure washing fleet trucks, mobile homes, or tractor-trailers (see Pressure Washing chapter for pricing).

If you personally lack the skill and/or the equipment to do any of the above and a vehicle comes in needing one of these things done, subcontract the work to a local service. A 20 to 30 percent markup for this is standard.

Final Tips

Plan on business cards. Remember to look sharp on those initial sales calls. However, instead of a suit and tie, you would do better if you wear a new uniform shirt with your company name and your first name on it. Also wear neat, pressed uniform pants. (Save the jeans for fishing.)

This is a good business, one that offers a feeling of satisfaction (besides the money you make) as you look at the dull used car you made look as good as your first used car you cleaned up to drive to school.

Carpet Cleaning

Many large cleaning service companies started out as carpet cleaners. It is an enjoyable trade. However, it is quite competitive in many areas. But then, what isn't today? In order to succeed, you must look for ways to rise above your competition.

There are several good methods available for commercial carpet cleaners. You may be sold on a particular type, but may find — as many have — that a combination of methods will be desirable. The reason for this is twofold: First, you can vary the methods used on carpet cleaned regularly. Dry foam can leave a slight residue that can build up over a period of time, and steam (hot water), depending on the psi and skill of the operator, can cause rot and over-wetting of the padding as well as the base of the carpet. Thus, some combine a program using these two methods. Second, you can offer what the customer prefers or what is best for that particular carpet.

Who Will Use My Service

- Homeowners

- Offices
- Restaurants
- Anyone with carpet.

What Is Involved

Your objective is to clean residential and commercial carpet better than your competition. Cleaning commercial carpet is often harder (particularly in restaurants), but offers more stability than residential customers once you have built up your business.

You will be dealing with many types of carpets and stains. Learning how best to deal with various types of stains takes some training but is not difficult to master. Suppliers are often eager to train you, providing you use their products.

Sales Manual

Include lots of pictures. Feature your equipment and before and after photos. Also include some businesses you clean, along with pictures of you and your crew — in uniform.

Insurance

You will need liability and bonding. (Note: Be aware that liability insurance does not cover performance. So if you ruin someone's carpet, you will not be covered.)

If you hire a crew, the usual employee-related insurances (unemployment and workers' compensation) will be needed too.

Equipment and Supplies

What you need depends on the way you clean carpet. There are several methods, some fairly new, and each has its strengths and weaknesses.

- Dry compound
- Dry foam
- Liquid dry cleaner
- Mist foam
- Shampoo detergent
- Water extraction (steam)

As discussed earlier, you may eventually want to use more than one method. New methods are coming out all the time. Many use dry foam machines on commercial accounts and then, every fourth time, use a portable hot water extraction (often called steam) method. The truck-mounted hot water extraction units are expensive but can be very profitable to use on volume residential and commercial work. Many carpet-cleaning units have attachments that will do a nice job on upholstery and drapery as well. These can be very profitable add-ons.

Cost of equipment can run from as low as $500 for a used unit to $3,000 and up for a new outfit. Truck-mounted hot water extraction units can vary from $2,500 to $5,000 used to $6,000 to $15,000 and up new, plus the cost of the truck.

Cost of chemicals and compounds is nominal compared to the dollar return per square foot. So buy the best. Also spend the extra few bucks for carpet protectors (small squares of vinyl or foil) to put under furniture after cleaning the carpet. Many of your competitors don't do this and they get complaints about staining.

Pricing

What does it pay? The current national average is a little over 20 cents per square foot. The days of 10 cents per square foot are or should be about gone, with the exception of large, commercial accounts. In such cases, you might bid as low as 9 cents in order to get 25,000 to 50,000 square feet at a time — or to please a current office cleaning customer.

The average price nationally for commercial work is much lower than residential due to its high volume. The national average for commercial is around 13 or 14 cents per square foot. But don't be afraid to try to get 15 to 20 cents for good quality work — perhaps highlighting that you are including a stain-retardant treatment.

Some carpet cleaning companies like to simplify and charge by the room. The cost is around $25 per room. (Some charge extra if they have to move furniture.) Homeowners seem to prefer this method, since they know beforehand about how much it will cost.

Finally, if you are unsure how you want to price your work, you can charge by the hour. Cost would be around $55 to $60 per hour for an operator and equipment.

Profitable Add-Ons

- Anti-static treatment priced around 9 cents per square foot

- Protective treatment at 4 to 8 cents per square foot

- Upholstery cleaning (see Smoke and Fire price list)

Final Tips

To build up your customer list, there are a number of things that have helped the successful companies. For one thing, follow the good business principles set forth in this book, most importantly your personal appearance. Be uniformed, clean in appearance, and friendly. Endeavor to put the customer at ease. Additionally, advertise, advertise, and advertise! Use the local cable TV channel, radio, small newspaper ads, Yellow Pages, and flyers with discount coupons left on all doors in a specific neighborhood. Also there are companies that send out packs of coupons. Have yours included. It will be worth the fee if you design a good coupon — again, offer a discount that has appeal. Become a member of the chamber of commerce or Better Business Bureau and include this fact in your advertising.

Ceiling Cleaning and Wall Washing

This specialty has come into its own in recent years. The tremendous use of acoustic ceiling tile and sprayed-on textured ceilings have created a need for a qualified person who can come in and clean these without destroying everything else in the room. These ceilings used to be difficult to clean.

Who Will Use My Service

- Homes and businesses of all types
- Offices
- Anyone with dirty walls or ceilings

What Is Involved

To clean ceilings, you go into a room or office and cover everything with plastic drop cloths. Then carefully clean the ceiling vents and the light fixtures. Next you will clean the entire ceiling using the spray method.

To clean walls, again use drop cloths. The traditional method is to use a cleaning solution in one bucket, a clear rinse solution in another, and then work from top to bottom. Because wall surfaces vary greatly and can look like one thing and really be another and the quality of paint and wallpapers differ, plan a test area for new surfaces. Judiciously wet wash a section that is inconspicuous. Follow with your rinse solution and finally wipe dry with a terry towel. Many prefer the new spray and wipe method, which uses machines to wet the walls. They aren't bad. You may prefer them, but after trying the machine approach, my company chose to stay with the handwash method. Again I must add, however, that there is much to be said for the new spray and wipe method.

In some cases, the chemical sponges that are used in smoke and fire restoration are good. However, in general, the newer spray system has become popular and profitable to use. Some include a bleaching agent. A nice development in recent years has been the enzyme-based cleaning solutions. The manufacturers claim these work without the normal (and sometimes harmful) bleaching or oxidizing. For walls, there are a number of good chemicals or powders for this, as well as some spray systems that do both ceilings and walls (again, using the new enzyme-based cleaning solutions).

As to training, some provide it free with equipment purchase. One leader in this field charges about $100 for a one-day seminar. (It is worth it.)

Sales Manual

Include references. Before and after pictures are especially effective. Include pictures of your ceiling and wall equipment, if you use it. Plus the manufacturers of these products will provide you with some excellent sales material to use.

Insurance

You will need liability and bonding; add employee-related insurance as your business grows.

Equipment and Supplies

If you chose to go with a wall-washing machine, you may drop $1,000 to $2,000 in it, or $4,000 for a complete outfit, including equipment and chemicals. Take your time with this particular decision. Your ceiling cleaning equipment can range from a $150 investment to $5,000 or more. The variance is due to the fact that you can do small jobs with a simple low pressure back-pack sprayer. As you get into the field you will quickly move up to a sprayer unit with an electric pump and some of the more sophisticated equipment designed to maximize the speed and quality of this basically simple job.

Chemicals. Wall cleaning powder and ceiling cleaning powder costs about $10 per pound. Liquid concentrate is priced at $70 to $80 per case of four gallons. (one gallon does about 700 square feet).

Pricing

For wet washing walls and chemical sponging ceilings, use the price list in the smoke and fire restoration section.

For spray-cleaning ceilings, the current rates are 15 to 25 cents per square foot. Price according to volume and difficulty. (For example, an old 16- to 20-foot bank ceiling will require the maximum price per square foot.) Add-ons can include window cleaning — see that section for pricing. The spray-cleaning method for walls is priced at 16 to 20 cents per square foot.

Profitable Add-Ons

- Office and home cleaning services
- Window cleaning
- Smoke/fire and water restoration
- Carpet cleaning

Final Tips

Neatness counts a lot in this business. Don't over-spray when using the wet method for ceilings. Use a painting edge or similar tool in tight areas. Don't underestimate the power of the chemicals. Be sure all furnishings, carpet, drapes, and, if necessary, walls are completely covered! Put everything back in order and get the customer's verbal (or written) approval of your work.

The amazing thing about the enzyme-based cleaners is what they can do for residential popcorn or sprayed ceilings. I used to believe the only way to restore these was to paint them, but these products do an excellent job even with this type of ceiling.

In heavily populated areas this could be a profitable, self-supporting business, not to mention an excellent part-time business. It is conceivable that a good operator working with a helper could make from $100 to $350 per hour. One company realized $600 to $700 per hour. Impressive! The rate depends on the experience of the operator and the number of obstacles in the operator's way.

Again, technology has opened up an excellent opportunity to do high-quality restoration work and make a doctor's income in this field.

Chimney Cleaning

An excellent opportunity for about $2,000 start-up cost is chimney cleaning. This is also a good add-on business for a smoke and fire restoration company. There are nearly 100 million chimneys and flues in the United States alone — all require cleaning. The public has gradually become aware of how important a periodic good cleaning is. Ideally, it should be done annually. Some laid-off or downsized executives as well as college students have done well with this.

Who Will Use My Service

Homeowners or anyone with a wood or coal burning fireplace or stove. Don't forget restaurants, inns, ski lodges, and other businesses with a wood-burning fireplace in the lobby or dining room.

What Is Involved

One popular method is using a powerful vacuum connected at the base of the chimney. Enclosing all around the fireplace opening so that no soot gets into the room, go up to the chimney top and select a wire brush that matches the shape of the flue. This wire brush is then inserted from the chimney top, using extension rods, until you have completely cleaned out the soot and creosote. The vacuum will pull it all out at the bottom. Some also use the brush with a weight on the end of a rope, and some opt for the safety of the ground and clean with the brush and extension rods from the fireplace.

New methods are gaining popularity in various parts of the country. Again, your equipment supplier will be a great help, eager to demonstrate what he or she has to offer.

Sales Manual

Include references and before and after photos. While scare tactics are in poor taste, some pictures of homes damaged by a chimney fire may help the homeowner see the value of your service.

Insurance

You will need liability and bonding. Workers' compensation and other employee-related coverage is particularly critical if you send workers up on the roof.

Equipment and Supplies

A 24- to 36-foot extension ladder, a safety harness, wire chimney brushes, extension rods, high performance soot vacuum, rope, weights, ridge hook, and plastic drop cloths. (A top hat is a nice touch.)

Pricing

Prices vary across the country, but $50 to $75 seems standard. You can discount $10 per chimney for two or more.

Profitable Add-Ons

If you are somewhat experienced in the trade, you can offer chimney repair as an add-on, or contract it out when you find a chimney needing more than cleaning.

With the growing popularity of gas log fireplaces and gas log inserts, you may wish to add the installation of these units, as well as wood-burning fireplace inserts. Price by the time spent, averaging at least $50 per hour.

Final Tips

Fall and early winter will in most cases be your peak season. You will work long hours at this time of the year once you are well established. Getting a listing in the local Yellow Pages will probably be your largest advertising investment and produce most of your business.

Get a little training. Be careful and don't slip off that roof! Although it is fairly simple work, it is wise to learn how to go about this efficiently and safely. The Appendix lists a number of sources for equipment and where to go for training. An efficient operator can do a chimney in 30 minutes to an hour. You can quickly see the potential for an organized operator to make a healthy income.

CHAPTER

19

Computer and Office Machine Cleaning

A specialized field that produces $50 or more per hour per operator has emerged in this high-tech age. With the number of computers in the world, the potential is awesome. Add to that the tremendous number of copiers and fax-phone systems. With a little training, many are going into large offices and cleaning the entire CPU unit. Some also include the under-the-floor wiring and overhead ceiling panels.

Don't be intimidated by the technology in this field. In many ways, a computer is like anything else that sits on the desk. It collects surface dust. It should be cleaned regularly. Unfortunately many computer owners and users are not yet aware of how important that is.

Who Will Use My Service

- Office buildings
- Any office, large or small, with a computer and/or office equipment
- Home offices

What Is Involved

There are different procedures for different machines. To simplify it, you perform a service whereby you carefully remove the equipment from its outer cabinet and clean the interior.

As this is merely an overview of this business, I am not going into a lot of depth about this excellent opportunity. If you are seriously interested, take one of the three-day basic training courses available in this field before you touch a machine.

Sales Manual

Your training will supply you with materials and statistics showing the powerful logic of having your potential customer's equipment regularly serviced by you.

Equipment and Supplies

A complete package including training, tools, equipment, supplies, hotel, and meals is currently being offered by a company in Texas for about $5,000.

Insurance

You will need liability, bonding, and employee-related insurance.

Pricing

To clean the average PC, for example, will take you 30 to 45 minutes. You will charge $45 to $70 for the service. At the other end of the spectrum, to go through a medium to large corporate clean room, it could take a crew of four to six about two to three days. You will need to provide meals and lodging for your crew if you are out of town. But your gross for a job that size would run between $10,000 and $20,000. Current pricing to clean a computer room or clean room floor is 18 to 22 cents per square foot.

Profitable Add-Ons

Profitable add-ons could inlcude maintaining the latest anti-virus program. Offer to check and clean up any viruses picked up over the Internet after you clean. Another service is to make a backup tape for them in case their system crashes someday.

Final Tips

I know some people in this business that are doing very well. They can afford to pay their help well above the average wage. However, it is wise to screen help carefully, selecting people who are conscientious and will carefully follow the procedures you require. There is no leeway for careless or sloppy workmanship in this field.

Concrete Cleaning and Sealing

A wise plant manager knows that, before using a new plant or addition, sealing the concrete floor with an acrylic or polyurethane sealer will save countless hours of floor maintenance in the future.

This is where you come in. It is an excellent diversification to a painting, plant cleaning, or floor service.

Who Will Use My Service

- New construction contractors
- Factories
- Warehouses
- Retail stores
- Garage owners

What Is Involved

You will go into an empty plant or sometimes one that has equipment. First you will clean-sweep and vacuum up debris. Then, depending on the condition and age of the concrete floor, run a large buffer (followed with mopping) or, better yet, a large auto-scrubber over the surface. Let it dry and then coat the floor with a concrete sealer or polyurethane product using a 24- to 32-ounce mop.

Sales Manual

One is not necessary for this business

Insurance

You will need liability and possibly bonding.

Equipment and Supplies

You will need 48-inch brooms and/or dust mops; a large propane buffer or a 32-inch auto-scrubber; 24- to 32-ounce mops, and large bucket and wringer.

Pricing

To clean old concrete, the cost is 35 to 45 cents per square foot (unobstructed).

For new concrete the price is 30 to 40 cents per square foot (unobstructed).

If there are machines or other items blocking your way, increase the price in proportion to the time lost. Add ten percent if you must do wet cleaning as well as dry in preparation for the finish.

Profitable Add-Ons

- Painting
- Waterproofing
- Floor maintenance
- Driveway cleaning and refinishing
- Cleaning and coating brick and ceramic tile floors

Final Tips

You can really cover a lot of square footage fast if you buy the finish in 30-gallon drums. Mount on a dolly or hand truck with a spigot at the lower end. Turn the spigot on to an appropriate volume and have one person pull it along. Then have a helper follow as it pours out, spreading it with a large mop.

A little math will give you an idea of how well you can do with a 100,000 square foot factory floor. Of course, as you get into these extra large jobs, you will have to compromise a bit on the pricing.

Graffiti Cleaning

A solid business, particularly in densely populated areas, is graffiti cleaning. It takes many forms. Vandals use spray paints, chalk, and even sharp instruments to deface various surfaces. This is a profitable specialty and a nice add-on for a painting or pressure washing service. Removing graffiti from walls, windows, concrete, brick, and stone is a growing service business.

Who Will Use My Service

- Building owners
- City governments
- Restaurants and other businesses with public restrooms
- Subway and bus lines

What Is Involved

In many cases, a good pressure washer will be all you need remove the graffiti without chemicals. Wooden benches and other wooden items used in public places may need wood filler, staining, and sanding. You will be on call by your prospective customers, because graffiti detracts from a business' image. Therefore, the sooner it is removed, the better. You may choose to wear a pager for this one (as well as many of the other service businesses).

Sales Manual

A sales manual would prove valuable, especially in getting established. Before and after pictures are powerful selling tools.

Insurance

Liability may be all you need if you work alone.

Equipment and Supplies

A 4,000 psi cold pressure washer or a 1,200 psi hot water pressure washer costs around $1,500. Some stiff brushes, ladders, and some chemicals are the only other tools you should need. Caution: Work closely with your janitorial supplier on the use of chemicals. Some do more harm than the graffiti. Always test an inconspicuous surface first — and wear protective clothing, gloves, and eyewear.

Pricing

- For repair and refinishing, use a rate of about $40 to $50 per hour.
- For pressure washing, use the rates as outlined in the section on pressure washing — you will want to set up a maintenance log and program as outlined there as well.
- For handwork, again due to the variety of tasks, try to average $40 to $50 per hour.
- On large jobs, chemicals should be billed as extras. In a number of cases repainting will be involved. (See the chapter on painting for pricing.)

Profitable Add-Ons

Painting and pressure washing services work well with this service.

Final Tips

Don't be in a hurry to use chemicals. Unless you are dealing with paint, first use plain water and let the pressure washer provide the muscle. If that doesn't work, try soap and water. If that doesn't work, try a citrus-based cleaner and water. If that doesn't work, try a lacquer thinner, and, finally, if you have to use paint remover or stripper, work from the outside of the affected area inward. This will reduce streaking and running. Apply chemicals to a rag or sponge, not directly to the surface. Sprayed-on chemicals may over-spray and run and may hurt other areas. Using a paint edge tool may protect surfaces in tight areas.

When you are finished there will be a real sense of satisfaction. You will feel good about yourself and your service when you finish a graffiti job.

Home Allergy Proofing

When I was growing up with allergies and asthma, I was in the minority. The idea of taking preventative measures to avert allergic attacks was unheard of, perhaps since the real causes of allergies were not fully understood.

Now, however, with pollution and other environmental factors, many people suffer from allergies and asthma to the point of frequent hospital stays and large medical bills. This has caused many frustrated people to seek help to prevent the outbreak of their sicknesses by removing the offending allergen from their environment — that is, from their homes. Health-conscious employers and school systems are also interested in improving their air quality, as well as preventing lawsuits and associated problems.

Since in an overwhelming number of cases the causes of the problem are dust, mold, and dust mites, it can require the kind of cleaning and organizing of a household that only a professional can accomplish. This is where you come in.

Who Will Use My Service

- Private homes

- Offices and workplaces

- Schools

- Day-care centers

What Is Involved

Be prepared to clean anything, especially in the air-handling systems. You can be most effective if the customer knows exactly what they are allergic to. Some things to look for when someone is sensitive to a particular allergen are as follows:

- *Dust.* Any clutter, newspapers, books, magazines, and carpeting; also check heat vents.

- *Dust mites.* Blinds, draperies, upholstered furniture, carpet, bedding, mattresses, pillows, and stuffed animals.

- *Dyes, glues.* Newspapers, books, and magazines.

- *Feathers.* Any feather or down pillows, comforters, or jackets.

- *Fumes/odors.* Varnish, paint, furniture, cleaning and laundry supplies, petroleum products, caulking, wallpaper glue, formaldehyde (new carpeting), air fresheners — solid or sprays.

- *Mildew/mold.* Under sinks, bathrooms, around windows and doors, basements, antiques, under refrigerators, closets, tile, plants, old books, forced air heating systems, attics, and heating/cooling ducts.

- *Pets.* Even if the pet has been removed, dander remains.

Procedures

- Inspect and then clean the ducts, if needed. (See Appendix for supplier of one of the new machines available for this procedure.)

- For mold removal use borax and water and coat ducts with an inhibitor. Sometimes mildew removal requires a two-stage procedure: Ammonia to kill mold and chlorine bleach to remove the stain. This must be done at least 24 hours apart, as ammonia and chlorine cause harmful vapors. This procedure can be used *only* if tolerated by allergy sufferer.

- Complete vacuuming from ceiling to floor, using vacuums equipped with high-quality micron filters.
- Change furnace and AC filters, replacing with new high-efficiency allergy filter. These are expensive, but washable. The manufacturer recommends monthly cleaning. But you may want to recommend the homeowner do so more often, if needed.
- Organizing clutter and removing as much as possible.
- Cover pillows, mattresses, box springs with *zippered* covers.
- Survey home environment to determine what will be needed to maintain control of allergens.

Sales Manual

Include statistics and illustrations from literature available on the subject from suppliers (listed in Appendix) and in books on the subject. The supplier of your duct-cleaning equipment, in particular, has some good material.

Insurance

You will need liability, bonding, and other employee-related insurances as you hire.

Equipment and Supplies

Your best problem-detection equipment will be a sensitive nose, coupled with a knowledge of allergies and their triggers.

- Acquire high efficiency particulate air filter (HEPA) vacuum cleaner.
- Stock environmentally-friendly and scent-free cleaners.
- Stock the more aggressive cleaners for when you cannot do the job with the above and the area can be aired thoroughly before the allergy sufferer returns.

Pricing

The cost of the special cleaning supplies for this work will be higher. However, most allergy sufferers do not mind this extra expense if it prevents further health problems. They may wish to purchase some of these chemicals from you for their own use later. Using the workloading system, price your service according to the time required at first, averaging $30 to $50 per hour for you and a helper, plus supply costs. You will charge much more than this rate when you clean the ducts. Your equipment supplier will be a big help to you when it comes to understanding the market for your area. When you are more comfortable with what you are doing, you will find the square foot system quicker and more profitable.

Profitable Add-Ons

After an initial cleaning, a weekly, monthly, or quarterly cleaning service will give you regular business. If the customer will sign an agreement, you can afford to figure at the $35 to $45 per hour rate. Also, a regular maid service can provide steady work in between major allergy seasons.

Final Tips

Leave your customer with a maintenance schedule to help keep the home as allergy-free as possible. The items you will include will vary greatly with each home. Some items you may need to evaluate are listed below.

- Washing methods for bedding
- Air filter replacement or cleaning schedule — for air cleaner and HVAC system
- Mold avoidance tips
- Cleaning and cleaning agents tips
- Products to use
- Humidity gauge
- Zippered encasings for box springs, mattresses, and pillows
- Vacuuming and dusting schedule

Floor Maintenance

This specialty is absolutely perfect for one person to operate. You don't need a fancy office — you can work right out of your home. This work gives many a great deal of satisfaction. Once you are comfortable handling the floor machine, the thinking person can enjoy doing just that. Then there is the satisfaction of seeing the good results of your work. A beautifully polished floor is a work of art.

Who Will Use My Service

- Retail stores
- Banks
- Malls
- Discount stores
- Grocery stores
- Restaurants

Many retail stores have tile floors. These are what this specialty targets. Specifically, the most desired clients are chain drug stores, chain discount stores, and chain food stores. (Caution with regard to food stores: There is more work per square foot than you will find elsewhere.)

Many of these chain stores are divided up into districts. A traveling district manager might cover 15 to 20 or more stores. Managers usually like to use the same contractor to do all the stores in their district, so growth can be fast if you do good work. When approaching the store manager of a chain, you can ask who the district manager is and how to get in touch.

What Is Involved

Using a high-speed buffer you may be required to buff a store's floors every one or two weeks. Then, using a low-speed buffer or auto-scrubber you may be expected to strip and refinish those floors once or twice a year.

The sweet part of this type of work is that the weekly buffing is usually done during the day or while the stores are open. This is one service business that allows you to be home at night — except for those times when you must strip the floors. The stores usually want stripping done after the store closes, often on a weekend.

Sales Manual

You probably won't need a sales manual, but you will need to provide references.

Insurance

You will need liability, bonding, and vehicle insurance.

Equipment and Supplies

A good used or new high-speed buffer is a good start. Most prefer the propane gas type because there are no cords to trip on. These, however, can be noisy and some produce a gas smell, which some customers may object to. Also, some stores may require you to use the electric high-speed machines. If you are taking on a chain of stores, be sure and find out before you start. The cost for a new buffer is $2,500 to $5,000, and used machines run $500 to $1,500.

An alternative to buying could be leasing one at between $90 to $140 per month, depending on the machine.

You will also need a low-speed buffer for when you strip the floors. The cost new is $1,000 to $1,500. You may rent one (17 to 20 inches) or do what I have done when getting started — keep checking the newspapers for good used ones. (By the way, invest in a splashguard for it. It will save you clean-up work.)

If you have the volume to justify it, you may want to look into an auto-scrubber. The cost ranges from $2,500 up to $10,000 or more. This sophisticated machine will put down the stripping solution, scrub, and then suck it back up again with its built-in wet vacuum, all in one pass.

Also you will want to consider a vehicle that can transport these sometimes very heavy pieces of equipment from store to store. A pickup or van will do. But you could also use a trailer. Ramps are a good back-saving investment too.

You will want to talk to one or preferably two janitorial suppliers in your area about the *best* floor stripper and the *best* high solids floor finish they sell. Don't skimp on either of these products. They will save you labor time.

You will also need a wet vacuum, mops, mop buckets and wringers (two), and some large dust mops. Also an edger (for floor stripping.)

Pricing

The charge for buffing is 1 to 1½ cents per square foot. This usually will involve a dust mopping, wet or damp mopping (where necessary), a high-speed buff, and one more quick dust mopping. The time to do a 4,000 to 5,000 square foot store using this procedure should be one to one-and-a-half hours for one operator. This produces a gross of around $40 per hour. Some customers like one recoat after the wet mop. Charge extra for this. An experienced operator can do four to six stores a day, producing around $200 to $300 gross.

Stripping runs 8 to 10 cents per square foot. The price usually includes stripping solution. When possible, bill floor finish in addition to this, but bill it at your cost. This work, usually done at night after store hours, will keep you up all that night, and you will need a hearty crew to help you. Most of us have done the stripping work, which is less profitable, so that we could get the more profitable daytime buffing work.

Profitable Add-Ons

- *Restrooms.* See the chapter on restroom cleaning and pricing.

- *Windows.* See the chapter on window cleaning and pricing.

Final Tips

Be sure you and employees (if you have them) look sharp and are friendly around people. Since you will be working around the store's customers, be observant of them and try to give them the right-of-way. Use safety signs and try to keep cords from places where people will trip on them. These safety tips are critical, because common accidents in stores are from people tripping or slipping. The liability in such a case would be yours. Therefore, have good insurance coverage, and do all you can to avoid accidents.

Finally, try to schedule as much of your floor stripping (after-hours work) and as little of your daytime buffing as possible around the holidays. Those stores get crowded at that time of year, which makes it difficult to work.

Landscaping Service

This is a term that applies to a number of related businesses. All are a pleasure for the person who enjoys working outdoors.

Who Will Use My Service

- Homeowners
- Businesses, large and small
- New construction sites

What Is Involved

For many, the entry level of this business is mowing grass, trimming shrubs and trees, mulching, edging, and the general maintenance of a yard. Perhaps we should refer to this specialty as Landscaping — Type A.

In its more advanced — and more profitable — form, however, landscaping services include the design, planting, and construction involved in the installation of a landscape property. This is Landscaping — Type B. Included in this field are plant growers and backhoe and bulldozer operators.

Type A is easy to get started with. Many support themselves in this way as they further their horticultural education and thus become able to move on to Type B services. This advanced service does require training, even if you have a green thumb. Most local community colleges offer courses inexpensively.

Sales Manual

For Type A, include pictures of especially attractive yards and properties you maintain or have maintained, as well as some references. The Type B manual could include attractive yards and projects you have designed and/or installed. Also show sample yard diagrams.

Insurance

You will need liability and possibly bonding — more as a sales tool than a needed insurance, however. Also when you begin to purchase expensive equipment, such as tractor lawn mowers, it would be wise to carry maintenance insurance. It's worth the $100 per year to protect a $5,000 mower.

Equipment and Supplies

For Type A you will need the following:

- A trailer with a drop gate for your equipment ($600 to $1,500)
- A push mower ($100 to $200)
- A good riding mower ($2,000 to $5,000). Some businesses get started with a $800 to $1,000 rider, but you will quickly need a heavy-duty machine
- A quality gas trimmer ($100 to $150)
- An edger ($100 to $150)
- A blower ($100 to $150)
- Rakes, shovels, etc. ($100+)
- Wheel barrow ($50 to $80)

For Type B, the most important equipment you will need will be between your ears. If you love plants and getting your hands in the earth; if you think you have a flair for exterior decorating; or if you enjoy learning about the plants indigenous to your area, with a little training you can be on your way to a lucrative career.

Pricing

For Type A, or a lawn service, I charged 50 cents an hour when I was ten years old. Those days are gone forever. Why, the kid down the street armed with only a simple push mower wants to average $15 to $25 per hour. For a full professional service, you need to average at least $40 to $50 per hour per person and equipment. Use this range (higher in most areas) as a guide to pricing Type A.

What you really want in this business is *yearly* contracts; and if you are dependable, both residential and commercial customers will agree to this. A full-service lawn and shrub contract, involving about four hours a week for a six-month season could run for the average half acre lot around $5,200. Add to this extra services, such as spring and fall yard cleaning, and you could increase it to $6,500 or $7,000. No work in the winter? Take a vacation, or look into snow removal.

For Type B service, involving design and installation, pricing is as diverse as the plants. In your initial projects, until you become more comfortable in your estimating, you may want to figure about $50 to $75 per hour for your services, plus a markup on plants, trees, and shrubs from a local nursery to cover the cost of selection, picking up, and planting. Most nurseries will replace plants that die, but the customer will expect you to care for that replacement.

As you grow in size and include the design and installation of a full landscape service, your financial rewards in many cases will surpass this hourly rate. To reach that point, though, you must have the credentials of formal training. Also get a copy of *Means Landscape Estimating*, Sylvia Hollman Fee, published by Construction Means Data Group Company.

Profitable Add-Ons

- Plant service (providing and caring for indoor plants — restaurants are a good customer for this)
- Parking lot cleaning
- Tree service
- Swimming pool service

Final Tips

A Type A landscape service is very easy to get started. However, only the operators who are professional, dependable, and honest survive. There seems to be more competition in the residential market than the commercial. So you may want to pursue the commercial aspect of this business — shopping centers, banks, or apartment complexes — as soon as possible.

One idea is to work hard during the warmer peak season for Type A service. Then use the off-season (or winter) to go to the local community college to learn design in order to qualify for the more advanced and lucrative Type B level of service.

If you love the outdoors and working with your hands, this may be the business for you.

Lighting Service

This service is absolutely one of the hottest business opportunities listed in this book. The following information is worth many times the cost of this book.

New technology in the lighting industry in the last five years has helped to contribute to the creation of this golden opportunity for diversification for any number of service businesses or, better yet, as a service industry in itself. Let me give you an example of what's happening.

A company in Connecticut asked a lighting manufacturer for help in reducing its light bill. An updated lighting system achieved a $9,000 per year reduction in energy costs. Better visibility contributed to a 7 percent rise in employee productivity and cut rejects by 40 percent.

Who Will Use My Service

- Factories
- Offices
- Banks

- Schools
- Retail stores

What Is Involved

By providing a light bulb changing and fixture clean-up service, you will be doing your customers a big favor. New technology in lighting, ballasts, dimming switches, occupancy sensors, etc., has created a wonderful opportunity. Another consideration is that offices where employees spend the day at a computer terminal need less lighting than offices of just five years ago. So downsizing the number of lights is necessary in such environments.

However, your main point in selling this unique service is that the savings for changing over to the new, better-engineered bulbs available today are phenomenal.

The savings by updating just *one* tungsten halogen lamp is up to $120 per year; one fluorescent lamp is $12 per year; and one HID lamp is $48 per year.

The new low-pressure sodium lamps are very energy efficient and yet give three times the light of mercury vapor lamps, watt for watt. As a result, one New York state manufacturer who spent $63,000 on the changeover recovered the entire amount in just three months! But please note — I am recommending not just bulb replacement, but cleaning the fixture and lens cover as well.

Can you afford a good ladder? Are you reasonably sure-footed climbing up and down it? Great! You are in business! You don't need to be a rocket scientist to do this. If you can read and follow a simple wiring diagram, you can do it.

It involves going into a building at a convenient time for the customer. That means second shift hours for most schools, colleges, or stores and third shift hours for most factories. Setting up your ladder or ladders, climb up, pull and clean the lens. Then pull out the old bulbs, clean the fixture, and replace the ballast and bulbs. One operator with (or in some cases without) a helper can do about four to six fixtures per hour.

Sales Manual

Following the sales principles outlined in Chapter 2 is important. Especially effective is the target principle. You may find that the sales representatives for lighting manufacturers can be a tremendous source for good leads. In most cases they are happy to help you, especially if you buy or have the customer buy their lighting items from them.

As you establish yourself, a sales manual is a must. Besides the normal information, include some statistics and some case histories of companies that have successfully re-lamped and how much they have saved. Again, your source for lighting can be a tremendous help in getting you the latest information. Some large lighting companies, even provide *free* training seminars. Take advantage of them.

Insurance

You will need liability and bonding for sure, and workers' compensation if you hire people to go up ladders for you.

Equipment and Supplies

As we have already said, there is very little equipment involved. You could use a few basic electrical tools, including a wire tester. (Caution: In case you run into a major electrical problem, don't take chances. Let a qualified electrician deal with that — either one the customer uses or one you could subcontract.)

As to ladders, you will find many facilities already have ladders and hydraulic lifts within the facility that they will let you use. They are often just the right height for their ceilings. But you may wish to invest in one or two good, sturdy, safe ladders, in case you go into that old bank building that has a ladder that should have been thrown out 20 years ago.

Don't invest in lighting supplies. When you make an initial building survey (often the light bulb representative will accompany you on a large sale), determine how many bulbs and starters you will need. Then simply have the supplier deliver them and bill the customer for them. Be sure this is stated in your initial proposal. This way you won't have to worry about getting stuck with a $20,000 bill for bulbs in the event a large customer changes his or her mind.

Pricing

This can and should be done very profitably. For example, to do a standard 48-inch four-bulb fluorescent fixture, you would charge $25 labor to clean and re-bulb. Additionally, you would replace the two old ballasts with *one* of the new type. The cost to the customer is about $25 for one of the new type, but the energy savings will justify it. Then you will replace the four bulbs with new ones. Customer cost for this is about $2 each.

To break this down, the customer will pay for an average four-bulb fixture:

> $25 for a new ballast
>
> $8 for four new bulbs
>
> $25 labor (for cleaning and re-lamping)

As mentioned, you should be able to do four to six units per hour (with or without a helper — depending on your physical condition and degree of manual dexterity. While working without a helper can increase profit, you could lose time and wear yourself out going up and down that ladder.) That will provide you a gross of $100 to $150 per hour. Other types of bulbs and fixtures will, of course, vary your price. But you should still average out at this hourly rate for your service or you have priced your re-lamping too low.

These figures work nicely if you are using an eight- to ten-foot stepladder or lift. But remember the principle mentioned earlier in pricing: the higher off the ground (or floor) you go, the higher the price goes. Logically then, for a 20- to 30-foot ceiling in a museum, library, or factory, you would have to *increase* rates in proportion to the increased labor time needed to get up to and from that height safely. Working at greater heights can also increase your insurance rates.

When re-lamping a large facility, it may be wise to offer on your proposal to do about 32 to 48 fixtures per night (normal height) or about 160 to 240 fixtures per week. By pacing yourself this way, you can keep your operation down to one or two people and thus maximize your overall profit for the job. The customer will be happy too, since payment for the entire job won't be due at one time.

Profitable Add-Ons

You don't need them. But this business could keep you busy when things get slow in seasonal service businesses (such as: painting, landscaping, smoke/fire or water restoration.)

Final Tips

Do not be disappointed or surprised if some large potential customers tell you that they do it themselves (in-house). That may be true or it may not. Most, however, have been having the janitor climb up and change a burnt-out bulb now and then. More than likely, that's what they are talking about. Even if they were to actually re-lamp their entire operation with these new low-energy bulbs and ballasts, they couldn't afford to assign the janitor the job for the next 12 months. They have too many other things on the schedule.

Your service is absolutely what they need. Don't ever forget that. If you don't convince him the first time, keep trying. Also, when you score a few of those early big jobs, get a letter of recommendation if possible from each of your customers and put it in your sales manual. Once some well-known local businesses go with this program, others will be more likely to want it too.

I am very enthused about this business. I just learned about it recently while helping to develop a maintenance program for a large facility. Now is the time to get into this. You will find most of your supplies can be obtained locally however, a Web site for a professional association is in the Appendix and may prove helpful.

Maid Service

As affluence increases and more households have two people working outside the home, the need for this service has mushroomed everywhere, not just in resort or wealthy areas.

The franchises that specialize in this service have had a phenomenal growth in the last decade. This indicates the market is ripe for an organized operator to pursue it. To succeed, the principles discussed in previous chapters will be of great help.

Who Will Use My Service

- Homeowners
- Resort property owners
- Landlords
- Resort rental agencies
- Real estate offices
- Private parties, weddings, etc.

What Is Involved

In a strong residential market, you will clean a client's home, usually once a week. The amount of work requested and size of the home will vary greatly, and these factors will determine your price. A major factor, indeed the key to succeeding at this business, will be your ability to be an organizer. Your crews will be small (two to four people) and fast. In fact, you will want to learn the new speed cleaning methods that have worked so well for the franchises. There are a couple of good books out on speed cleaning. Read them.

More than any other of the service businesses, this business often grows quickly through referrals. If you do a good job, the home or apartment owner will tell others. They, too, will want your services, and so it grows. If you want to encourage this, you might ask a satisfied customer if anyone he or she knows would like your service. Give them a few of your business cards to share with friends.

You will want to advertise in the Yellow Pages, use flyers, local cable TV, small newspaper ads, and radio. Don't hesitate to use coupons. Perhaps your local chamber of commerce has a display area where they will allow you to leave some of your business cards or advertising material for newcomers to the area. Buy bonding insurance and advertise this fact.

This business has helped to make some people *very well off!*

Sales Manual

Include pictures of you and your crew in uniform — holding vacuums and feather dusters. References are always important. Look for areas where you and your people excel and highlight these (i.e., "We do windows!").

Also use a simple agreement, indicating what is to be done and how often. Include a sample of this agreement in your manual.

Insurance

You will need liability, bonding, and other employee-related insurances as you hire.

Equipment and Supplies

Get a number of 12 to 18 amp upright vacuums, which should run $125 to $200 each. A good canister vacuum is $100 to $300. You may be able to obtain a used 12- to 15-inch buffer costing $50+. A new one will run $500 to $700. Rags, mops, buckets, and some specialized cleaning supplies such as carpet spot remover or gum remover are also required. However, most maid services do not provide cleaning chemicals, paper products, garbage bag liners, etc. A list of needs is left with the customer or they can be provided, the cost with included in the bill.

You can start the business with just a few hundred dollars by using some of your own equipment from home. But plan on at least $1,000+ initial outlay if you have to buy.

Pricing

Pricing varies considerably from one area to another. Generally the average price nationally for a typical three-bedroom house is $60 to $75 per visit. Some in California are getting $85 to $120 and in some areas of the Southeast, only $35 to $50.

How can you distinguish yourself, get good jobs in spite of competition, and get your price? Naturally you will get a better price if your crews look professional, with uniform shirts or blouses, and do quality work. Another important consideration is a comprehensive pricing method. The franchises have mastered this well. Have a price list that includes figures for all the extras, such as oven cleaning, windows, dish washing, floor stripping, and ironing. *It is a simple process to develop a good price list.* Simply do each one of these projects once yourself and time it. Figure on the basis of $30 per hour for one person and equipment, including the time to get to and from the job. Then calculate. For example, if it takes you a half an hour to clean the inside of an average refrigerator, figure on $15. After you work up this list, you might issue a copy to each crew chief and keep a copy near the phone. If you have a professional pricing system, it will discourage the problem of homeowners wanting freebies, which can kill your profit margin.

Profitable Add-Ons

There are a number of specialty add-ons that you may consider.

- Window washing
- Pressure washing homes and driveways
- Painting
- House/pet/plant sitting

- Minor repairs

- Construction cleanup

- Arranging for parties (caterers, music, flowers, etc.)

Final Tips

Besides sharp uniforms, endeavor to choose clean-cut people who will put the homeowner at ease. Be sure they leave for the job with neat, organized equipment. Endeavor to select crew chiefs with people skills, or take some time to train them.

Everyone working with you will need to learn to notice details (i.e., fingerprints and smudges on light switches) and perhaps add that extra little touch. Think about how you notice things, like when you check into a hotel and the toilet paper roll has the ends turned in, or there's a mint on the pillow. How much effort did that take? Almost none. Well, the homeowner will notice little special touches too.

New Construction Clean-Up

Have you ever seen a carpenter, plumber, or an electrician who cleaned up after finishing a job? The very few who do would rather not, and clean-up is usually superficial at best. This type of service is really in demand.

Who Will Use My Service

- Home improvement and construction companies
- Real estate companies
- Homeowners and landlords

What Is Involved

Much of what is involved in an apartment prep service will lend itself to this. In addition to the final clean-up of a house, apartment, condominium, or business building when the construction workers are all through, you may be required to pressure wash portions of the exteriors (see chapter on pressure washing). You may even need to use muriatic acid or pressure wash the brick work (protective glasses and gloves are a must).

Sales Manual

Not necessary.

Insurance

Only liability is a must, until you begin to hire help.

Equipment and Supplies

See chapters on apartment prep service and pressure washing.

Pricing

Per 1,000 square feet, the price usually runs from $75 to $150, depending on the amount of dirt and debris left behind by the construction workers Add to that windows (see windows chapter for pricing — be sure to price windows on the high end due to the amount of razor scraping needed). If exterior work such as pressure washing is needed, see pricing under that section.

As you are established with a contractor, you may contract for a set price based on the above. Include payment for surprises in your agreement. For example, you walk into a living room to clean and there you see 24 pieces of 4' x 12' sheet rock that must be carried to the garage by two people before you can even start to clean. Another common situation is that you clean an area, but a painter or carpenter comes back in to finish up something and in the process messes up all you have done. It is not uncommon for you to have to clean some areas more than once. Your pricing must reflect that if you are going to stay in business.

Profitable Add-Ons

Depending on the economy and the amount of building going on in your area, this can make a business in itself. It can also blend well with the following:

- Janitorial service
- Maid service
- Apartment prep service
- Painting
- Landscaping

- House sitting

- Minor repairs

Final Tips

Be sure you have the billing terms clearly spelled out as to when you get paid. Money can be hard to collect unless you work with good contractors. You will often find you are working under a deadline. Once you establish yourself with reliable contractors with years of successful building experience, they will keep you busy.

Look for large commercial building construction jobs, such as schools. These can be very profitable. In some cases, these companies clean up themselves, but now more of them contract it out, knowing they usually get a better job with fewer headaches. In fact, many are so eager to find a reliable contractor, they will pay premium rates to one that they find can be depended upon.

Office Cleaning

You will note more space is devoted to this specialty than any of the others in this book. That is because more fortunes have been made from this one than any of the others. Indeed, there is some very serious money to be made in this easy-to-start-up business.

Many who start a cleaning business of any type often find that, as they grow, office cleaning becomes the most desirable. There are a number of reasons for this.

When you work in a private home, people can be very picky about how their home is maintained. Some housewives like to stand over you to see that you are doing the job correctly. This is not to say that many office managers are not picky, too. But you are dealing with a professional person, and in most cases, you are there at a time when no one is standing over you inspecting as you work. Therefore, if you have missed something, you can go back and get it on your final inspection before leaving.

Another reason is that the work is usually steady. You know you will be cleaning the offices of ABC Company every Monday, Wednesday, and Friday night.

You know it should take a little over two hours to do each time. And, best of all, you know you have an agreed-upon payment coming in at the end of the week or month.

Who Will Use My Service

Almost every business has an office. Of course, to be profitable, you will always look for the offices of substantial size.

What Is Involved

Getting the first account may take some time. It may take you accepting one-time clean-up jobs or window-cleaning jobs for offices. However, as outlined earlier, I can't overemphasize the value of a sharp, neat, and clean appearance. You want these people to give you the keys to their building. You have to look like you can be trusted with them.

Most will put you off or even say no on your first call, but don't let that deter you. The next time you call, you will be a familiar face and perhaps you will have a chance to bid.

As to the performance skills required, if you read the other service business chapters in this book and put them all together, you get an idea of what is required. You will need to know how to clean and dust, clean carpet, wash windows, maintain restrooms — you get the idea. Over the years in my office cleaning business, there isn't much that I haven't been called on to do. When I didn't know how to do something, I found someone who did and hired that person on until I could learn myself. In addition, I sought out a good book on the subject.

Sales Manual

You will definitely need one that includes references and pictures of workers in uniform. In the chapter about restroom cleaning, there is some information about bacteria that is found in the bathroom. This can be useful as a sales tool and should be included.

Insurance

You will need liability and bonding. As you add employees, get unemployment, workers' compensation, and perhaps a health plan.

Equipment and Supplies

Usually a good upright or canister vacuum and a used buffer will get you started. Buy only what you need for a specific job.

As to supplies, shop for a good deal on basic supplies. Sometimes the best place to find things such as cleanser, toilet brushes, and brooms is a discount store. When you grow enough to order caseloads or need a truly industrial strength product, shop for a good janitorial supplier. Some basic needs to start with are as follows:

- Upright vacuum (12 to 18 amps motor). A discount store sells them for $125 to $200.

- Low-speed buffer, about 15 to 21 inches. Look for a used one in good condition, and try to buy brand names. Check classified ads and look in older department stores or paint and hardware stores. Some may have one in back they do not use any more. Your goal is to leave a buffer on each job, rather than getting a hernia lugging one around.

- A wet vacuum for picking up liquids and for wet surfaces. Buy it new from discount stores; the plastic five- to ten-gallon size run $50 to $75.

- A mop bucket and wringer. The 26-quart size can be purchased at grocery or janitorial supply companies for $60 to $90.

- Wet mops. Minimum requirement is two 36-ounce mop heads and handles, if you are strong; or two 24-ounce mop heads and handles if you are not. They cost $25 to $35.

- Window-washing equipment. Buy new and best quality, probably from a janitorial supplier. Complete basic set-up is $100 to $300.

- Trash can on wheels — largest you can get. It should cost $30 to $60.

- Dust mops. Minimum two 24-inch dust mop heads, frames, and handles for $25 to $35.

- Brooms, pails, brushes, rubber gloves, dust cloths, etc., for $50.

- Cleaners, which include:
    - Carpet spot remover   – Furniture polish   – Floor stripper*
    - Disinfectant glass cleaner   – All-purpose cleaner   – Floor finish*

    * When starting out, buy at a janitorial supplier the day before you are going to use the products.

- Carpet cleaners — Start out by renting, then decide on a system you want to buy.

On a budget, basic equipment start-up cost will run from approximately $600 to $1,270. If you have the investment money and want to go first-class, you can expand your line with more of the above. You can look into a high-speed buffer; a 20-gallon fiberglass wet vacuum; and purchase a hot-water extraction and/or dry foam carpet cleaner. A van with your company name painted on it is a nice touch too.

Pricing

As discussed earlier, two basic systems — the square-foot and workload systems — will help you determine how much to charge for the office you need to clean. Don't be the cheapest. Those who bid very low often promise more than they can do for the money. They then cut corners and end up out of business. Keep your word, and your reputation will make you worth your price.

Profitable Add-Ons

There are many ways to increase your office-cleaning contract. Do they have parking lots that need cleaning? The ceilings and walls need cleaning. Those fluorescent light fixtures may need upgrading and changing. Carpet cleaning is often a good add-on. If you are truly innovative, you can add terrazzo or stone cleaning, pest control, landscaping service, and even security guard service. In fact, most service businesses listed in this book will have some application to this type of specialty. Look through them for ideas.

Final Tips

Because the janitorial/office cleaning business is one of the more complex and all-inclusive service businesses, it is used as an example on the sample forms in this chapter.

The estimate schedule, Figure 28.1, is the backbone of your proposal. Forms can be purchased with similar format or you can custom tailor your own. Use the form on your initial survey to mark down what needs to be done and how often the customer wants it done. Then use the form as a wall chart or job schedule to remind your employees of the tasks that need to be done on that job and when they are to be done.

Figures 28.2 through 28.5 would apply in a large facility to standardize work procedures. They cover the basics and serve as a tutor for new employees and a reminder to the existing staff.

As you grow, you may find you have a tiger by the tail. The potential for growth is endless. But by using your head, this business can be profitable yet allow you time to enjoy life. The office cleaning business can give you the stability of an above-average regular income that only improves with time.

FIGURE 28.1: Estimate/Cleaning Schedule

Company: _____ Area: _____ Contact: _____							
Weekly Tasks	Mon	Tue	Wed	Thu	Fri	Sat	Sun
General:							
Entrance: Sweep sidewalk							
Entrance: Clean glass doors							
Police entrance/parking area for loose debris							
High Dusting: Light fixtures, vents, etc.							
Trash cans, ash trays, sand urns: Empty/Clean							
Dust: Furniture, desks, counters, tables, files, window sills, etc.							
Clean: Counters, break areas, water fountains							
Clean: Bright metal work — handles, plates							
Water plants							
Vacuum furniture, upholstery/drapery							
Floors:							
Vacuum carpeting — high traffic/entrance							
Vacuum carpeting — thorough							
Sweep/dust mop hard floors							
Mop hard floors							
Spray/buff hard floors							
Restrooms:							
Clean: Mirrors, bright work							
Clean/disinfect: Counters, sinks, toilets, urinals							
Empty trash and waste containers							
Clean: Partitions, tile areas							
Refill dispensers: Soap, TP, towels, vending							
Sweep floor							
Mop/disinfect floor							
Windows:							
Outside							
Inside							
Entrance area							
Other:							
Other Services (estimate on request)							
Frequency per year .							
Carpet cleaning							
Strip and reseal floors							
Wash light fixtures							
Change light bulbs							
Wash/clean walls							
Wash/clean ceilings							
Clean vent grills, ducts							
Clean upholstery/drapery							
Clean/disinfect trash cans/waste receptacles							
Pressure clean parking lot, outside building, dumpsters, etc.							
All Areas: Every Work Night:							
Inspect work							
Make security and light check							

FIGURE 28.2: How to Dust and Clean

How to Dust and Clean

1. **SAFETY FIRST.** Do your high dusting first.
   Where possible, use extendible dusters.
   Avoid standing on chairs to reach.

2. **Check your supplies.** You will need:

   - a duster

   - a spray bottle of all-purpose cleaner

   - some clean cloths

3. **Always start high and work down.** Start at the right of the doorway and work a complete circle. After doing high dusting:

   - *Desks.* Dust higher surfaces (shelves & file cabinets) first. Dust back and forth over surface until entire surface has been cleaned. Dust knee hole with a hand duster. Move objects to dust under them.

   - *Chairs/seats.* Dust from top down. Use hand duster for legs and bottoms when practical.

   - *Halls/walls/auditoriums.* Dust fire doors, fire extinguishers, exit signs, molding, bars on exit doors, any horizontal surface. Be observant.

4. **Wherever you encounter *stainless steel* (door plates, restrooms, etc.) use only containers marked as stainless steel cleaner.**

   - Spray

   - Wipe

   - Wipe again with clean cloth

   - Be careful not to get stainless steel cleaner on any other surface. Immediately remove if it comes in contact with wood or other surfaces.

5. **When cleaning *wood* (doors, furniture, etc.) use only furniture cleaner. Spray on cloth and wipe.**

6. **When finished, *inspect* your work, then return cleaning materials to storage area.** Dispose of paper.

FIGURE 28.3: How to Clean Restrooms

How to Clean Restrooms

1. **SAFETY FIRST.**

   - Put on rubber gloves

   - Check on and report in writing any leaking faucets or toilets

2. **Use disinfectant cleaner to clean all counters, stall handles, urinals, and toilet seats (after cleaning put seat down).** Let cleaner remain on the above for at least a few minutes before wiping.

   - Inside urinals and toilets use bowl brush (spray disinfectant cleaner liberally inside and leave it there)

   - Use a sponge on the outside of the fixtures

   - Thoroughly clean underside of toilet seat as well as top

3. **Refill soap, towel, and toilet tissue dispensers.** (Do not place extra rolls of toilet tissue in rest room unless instructed to do so.)

4. **Wipe fingerprints off mirrors with a paper towel and glass cleaner.**

5. **Empty all trash receptacles:**

   - This includes liners, which you will replace with new ones

   - Check and empty all sanitary napkin receptacles, including liners, which you will replace with new liners

6. **Clean all stainless steel with stainless steel cleaner.** (Use moderately.) Follow instructions under *How to Dust and Clean* (Item #4).

7. **Sweep and then wet mop according to instructions under *How to Mop*.**

8. **Check entire restroom for cleanliness before leaving and after the floors are dry**.

FIGURE 28.4: How to Mop

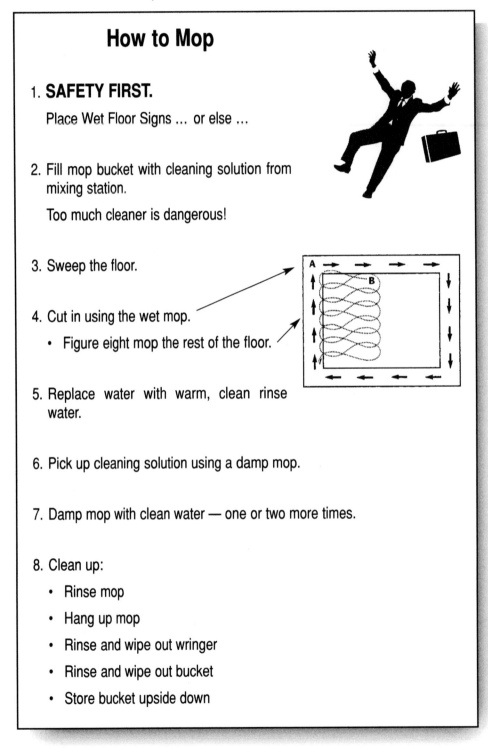

How to Mop

1. **SAFETY FIRST.**

   Place Wet Floor Signs ... or else ...

2. Fill mop bucket with cleaning solution from mixing station.

   Too much cleaner is dangerous!

3. Sweep the floor.

4. Cut in using the wet mop.

   • Figure eight mop the rest of the floor.

5. Replace water with warm, clean rinse water.

6. Pick up cleaning solution using a damp mop.

7. Damp mop with clean water — one or two more times.

8. Clean up:

   • Rinse mop

   • Hang up mop

   • Rinse and wipe out wringer

   • Rinse and wipe out bucket

   • Store bucket upside down

FIGURE 28.5: How to Vacuum

How to Vacuum

1. **SAFETY FIRST.**

   Check your equipment

   - Is your equipment in good shape? Does the electric cord look good?

   - Has the vacuum bag been emptied? (A bag ¼ full, or less, reduces cleaning by 50%.)

   - When you plug in your vacuum, only one vacuum per electrical outlet

   - Never jerk your plug out of the socket by pulling cord

2. Plug in vacuum (be sure the switch is in the off position).

3. When using a **standard upright**, stand in one place and use a back-and-forth movement. Standard upright vacuums are not designed to walk behind. Also be careful not to bump against walls, seats, or desks.

4. When using a **canister** (or back-pack) type, use it for vacuuming the edges of the carpet, under desks, between seats and carpeted walls in the auditorium.

5. When using a **large upright**, designed for the lobby, halls, or large open areas, always watch ahead at all times. Since these vacuums (unlike the small, upright vacuums) are designed to walk behind, watch your cord. Stop and unplug before you reach the limit of your cord.

6. When finished, carefully **empty your vacuum bag** into a trash can, being careful not to spread dust. Wipe down vacuum and return it to the designated storage closet.

Painting

Painting is one of the more personally satisfying of the service businesses, but not everyone qualifies to be a professional.

Do you have reasonable manual dexterity? Are you careful to do neat work fast enough to be productive? Do you have reasonable common sense and stay sober? Then you probably can make it in this field.

The franchises evidently feel this service is a good one, as they now sell franchises for it. They are right about one thing — it is a profession that can do well if it's properly organized.

Who Will Use My Service

- Homeowners
- Retail stores
- Businesses, large and small
- City water companies (water towers)

- Smoke/fire and water restoration businesses

What Is Involved

Painting! Simple? Not really. Painting houses, buildings (inside or outside), water towers, etc., involves a great variety of techniques and equipment.

If you are contracted to paint the outside of a house, here's where common sense comes in. Think of what you would want if it were your house. Cover any shrubs and plants with drop cloths, taking care not to damage them. Set up either a ladder or scaffold. Do your main areas first and then come back and trim. Watch around windows — use an edging tool to save time, because neatness counts.

If you were to paint a cinder block wall on a shopping center, you would probably use one of the new airless sprayers. A sprayed ceiling in a house would require a deep roller on an extension pole (there are even devices to catch drips).

Obviously, what is involved will vary with the type of job.

Sales Manual

Put together a sales manual with references and before and after pictures. You might include paint chip samples of some fancy work you do.

Insurance

You will need liability and vehicle coverage for a work truck.

Equipment and Supplies

- *Brushes.* Buy only the absolute best quality that you can find and clean them properly after each day's use.

- *Rollers.* Regular and deep nap with three, four, and six- to ten-foot expandable extension handles.

- *Ladders.* Fiberglass — both step and extension types.

- *Scaffolding.* Safer than ladders. The type needed depends on your market.

- *Drop cloths.* Some large cloths, but a lot of three to four mil plastic (buy it by the 100-foot roll).

- *Sprayers.* A good one-third to one-half horsepower airless sprayer to start with.

- *Transportation.* A lot of small operators use what they call their paint wagon: That is, an older station wagon or van for hauling their supplies. Get it lettered with your company name and phone number, or invest in magnetic signs.

Pricing

The following pricing has worked in most areas. Your area market may vary somewhat.

Interior:	One coat is 12 cents per square foot, plus paint.
	Two coats are 18 cents per square foot, plus paint.
Exterior:	One coat is 18 cents per square foot, plus paint.
	Two coats are 24 cents per square foot, plus paint.
Exterior Spray:	10 to 18 cents per square foot, plus paint.
Water Towers:	$150 to $225 per hour, plus paint. (Remember the height rule mentioned earlier.)
Interior Kitchen Cabinets:	$.75 to $1.25 per square foot for prep and labor, plus paint or stain.
Roofs:	25 cents per square foot, plus paint or linseed oil.

Profitable Add-Ons

- Waterproofing treatment for basements
- Repainting swimming pools
- Treatment of smoke-damaged surfaces
- Sign painting

Final Tips

Painting is great work. The principles for running a good operation are the same as the other service businesses we have discussed. There are some painters

I know who just don't like to estimate. So they have a price of $10 to $20 or more per hour per painter. The honest ones I know who are doing that have a backlog of work for 12 months.

Parking Lot Cleaning

In my work as a consultant, I helped a young man start out in this field about ten years ago. He quickly moved up to a large, truck-mounted unit and quit his job in a grocery store. His operation grew from a $1,500 investment to a $120,000 a year one-man operation. Today he is financially independent and has a great business. Don't be afraid to grow, but always try to get the accounts before you invest in the equipment — at least to a reasonable degree.

Who Will Use My Service

Anyone with a parking lot. Some prospects include the following:

- Shopping centers

- Hospitals, medical facilities

- Office complexes

- Banks, stores, service stations with a private parking lot

- Parking garages and decks

- Airports
- Warehouses and seaports

What Is Involved

This service is so much in demand in some areas, just riding around town in your truck could get customers. But to get the choice accounts, you may wish to use the target approach to obtain the big parking lots that will produce a regular income.

How often do you want to clean a parking lot? Some shopping centers will want your service five to seven nights per week. A hospital may only want one or two times per month — establish a minimum of at least once per month for any account.

It would be best if you and your customer sign a contract or agreement. Legal help with the wording is recommended, particularly as you start out. The sample in the first section of this book will give you some guidelines as to what should be included. There are often misunderstandings in this field when it is not in writing. Be sure to include all details in the contract. Also, if possible, negotiate to have a large account provide you with a dedicated on-site dumpster and put this in the contract too.

Equipment and Supplies

To care for my customers' facilities under contract, my company has used a $1,500 gasoline-operated Billy Goat™ or vacuum. Combined with some detail sweeping on curbs, these do a nice job. But to get into this as a main business, you will want to eventually go to a truck-mounted air sweeper and vacuum. These trucks can pick up two and a half yards of debris as they sweep. If you are planning to clean the parking lots for a large company or shopping center, a truck like this is a must. Also, the mechanical truck-mounted sweepers are fast. They can carry up to four yards of debris and have self-contained water systems to cut down on the dust. Cost for a rider is $8,000 to $10,000 and $65,000+ for a good truck-mount unit.

More than likely, the equipment manufacturer's representative will gladly fill in any other details or questions you have.

This business is good for an operator who wants a very profitable one- or two-person operation.

Insurance

You will need liability and insurance for your vehicle and employee-related insurances, if you hire help.

Sales Manual

When you develop a sales manual for this business, be sure to include some information from the federal Environmental Protection Agency (EPA) that show they approve and, in fact, recommend these forms of maintenance under the Best Management Practice (BMP) principle. Have your truck professionally lettered and then maintain it in immaculate condition. Put a picture of your outfit on the first page of the sales manual.

Another selling point for your sales manual is that regular parking lot sweeping will reduce the need (in some cases) for some of the inside maintenance. It reduces the grit and sand that is tracked in.

Pricing

One person and a truck-mounted sweeper vary from $1.00 to $1.60 *per minute*. If you low bid $240, for example, it means you plan on spending about three to four hours on the job. Also, when you have an account that only gets it done twice a year, you will probably need to charge your maximum rate.

Profitable Add-Ons

- Sweep sidewalks and remove trash from outside grounds. Initial sweep jobs or one-time sweeps are usually a lot more work. You may need to charge a bit more for these. Also be aware if there are any noise curfews to work around.

- Sidewalks and concrete parking lots need periodic cleaning with a pressure washer. Depending on the volume of work, you could rent or buy a pressure washer for this. (See Chapter 32.)

Final Tips

If you come after hours or weekends as most in this business must, you might become invisible to your customer. Therefore, your daytime PR work with your customers will keep you ahead of the competition.

This is an excellent business for an operator that wants to keep less than four employees, and thus minimize employee-related expenses and headaches. The major expense is in equipment, rather than labor, and the business can even be run out of your home.

Pest Control Service

An older and profitable service business that has survived with a good profit margin in spite of the competition is the pest control service. In many areas it will require a license and certification, but they are not difficult to obtain. You will also want to get training from the pesticide manufacturer or at one of the seminars that are available.

Who Will Use My Service

- Homeowners
- Apartment management agencies
- Realtors
- Businesses of all types, especially where there is food

What Is Involved

Residential pest control usually involves a termite treatment contract (very profitable). A basic comprehensive treatment, depending on the climate, should last from 5 to 20 years, unless something happens that compromises structural barriers. Then you follow up with a yearly inspection at a fee stipulated in the original contract. If you are a homeowner yourself, you are already familiar with the extent of the treatment needed in your area.

Other bug treatments may involve a nice monthly contract — particularly when dealing with apartments. Also, be prepared for calls to get rid of rats, mice, snakes, deer, rabbits, squirrels or — in the area I live — 400-pound wild pigs (tearing up gardens) and alligators (that's right, I said *alligators*).

Commercial business offers some nice volume. Plant or office buildings as well as all types of stores and restaurants need this service.

You would usually spray your chemicals with a portable low-pressure sprayer, but be prepared to use a gasoline-powered low-pressure sprayer mounted on your pickup truck.

Insurance

Liability, vehicle insurance, and bonding are musts.

Equipment and Supplies

You will need portable sprayers, a truck-mount sprayer, and a 30- to 50-gallon tank. Also you will use a half-horsepower electric contractors' drill with extension bits.

Depending on what size pests you deal with, you may eventually get some wire humane traps. Chemicals are diversified according to state regulations and what you are going after. Talk with your local supplier.

Start-up costs run about $5,000 to $8,000 plus truck and training.

Pricing

Residential. To give a house a basic first-time termite treatment is $1,000 to $1,500. I have watched a crew of three do this in two hours or less. Yearly touch-up is $75 to $150.

Monthly ant and roach treatment is $50 to $75 or more per month. For larger pests you should negotiate.

Commercial. A 4,000-square-foot store is $35 to $50 per monthly touch up. (I've seen this done in 10 to15 minutes, because only certain critical areas are treated.) Price larger accounts according to your hourly worth and the competition. In many areas, $50 to $100 per hour is competitive.

Profitable Add-Ons

Not much needs to be added to this profitable business, but you could offer home allergy treatment.

Speaking of allergy sufferers, they often forego pest control treatment because they cannot tolerate the strong chemicals. As the industry becomes more and more aware of this problem, environmentally friendly treatments are being researched and offered to some extent. If you can keep abreast with the latest technology and chemicals being developed, you may open a whole new market for yourself.

Final Tips

As mentioned earlier, training is important. Considering the current sensitivity people have about insecticides, you need to be properly informed and qualified; and you will need to continue to stay up-to-date on the latest information about the chemicals being used. However, this doesn't take long to do.

Although there is a lot of money made in this field, there is a lot of responsibility too. For example, when you treat a house, the industry standard is to provide a large termite damage insurance policy. For commercial work, you will pay special attention to breakrooms and dumpster areas — anywhere food residue is found. Also bathrooms attract bugs through the plumbing openings and due to the attraction of standing water. Many of these principles apply to residential treatment as well.

If you look neat and do a complete job, you will be able to compete successfully with the giants in this business.

32

Pressure Washing

With just a few thousand dollars in equipment and an old, used pickup truck, an operator in North Carolina I know makes $1,000 a day cleaning old buildings that are being restored. However, if you only did one fourth of that, I would say you had a decent day. This is an excellent, low-investment business.

Who Will Use My Service

- Homeowners: Houses, siding, including roofs and cedar siding, driveways
- Building owners
- Businesses with fleets of trucks
- Parking lot owners especially for curbs and sidewalks
- Service station owners
- Mobile home owners
- Restaurants: Hoods, grease filters, and ducts
- Supermarkets, for carts (very profitable)

- Loading dock businesses, for dumpsters and awnings
- Contractors for new construction, commercial buildings cleanup
- Anyone needing graffiti removed

What Is Involved

The market in this rapid-growth industry is exploding. This is an excellent home-based business that you can start with a relatively low initial investment.

Your bread-and-butter accounts will be the regular customers you want to put on a weekly, semi-monthly, or monthly schedule. Fleet trucks and supermarket chains are the prime customers. Then you can supplement your business with the gravy, that is, the large or small one-time customers.

This would be a great business for a young student going through college because of its low investment, and overhead and flexible hours.

Sales Manual

Be sure to include before and after shots of buildings you have done and references.

Insurance

Liability may be all you need. Add employee-related insurances if you hire help. You will want coverage for your work vehicle.

Equipment and Supplies

An investment as low as $600 for a 2,000 psi cold-water machine, or up to $2,000 for a 4,000 psi cold-water machine, will put you in business. I personally use the 4,000 psi machines, which do a tremendous job. I am currently paying around $1,600 per unit for mine. You can always reduce the pressure on a 4,000 psi if you need to (i.e., for cedar shakes), but you can't increase the pressure on a smaller unit beyond its maximum rating. You can get machines that crank out up to 10,000 psi, some on their own trailer. Plus some models heat the water and a few even produce steam.

If you do not have a suitable vehicle, such as a pickup or van, this could be an added expenditure. However, a 4 x 8 utility trailer with your equipment mounted on it works fine. Just haul it around with your car.

Pricing

For a high-volume account under contract, I have gone as low as $35 per hour, but $50 to $90 is more appropriate. Factoring in the difficulty level of the work, such as climbing a ladder, would raise that price.

A fixed-rate price list will not only help you, but also give you a more professional image. You will be wise to check what is reasonable for your locality, but here is a sample price list.

- *Trucks.* Small are $5 to $10; large from $15 to $35.

- *Mobile homes.* $1.50 per running foot.

- *Houses.* 10 to 12 cents per square foot (first floor or ground level); 20 to 22 cents per square foot (second floor). The higher you climb, the higher the price.

- *Parking lots.* 5 to 12 cents per square foot (depends on the condition of the concrete). If acid is used, 25 to 30 cents per square foot.

- *Restaurant hoods and ducts.* Small are $100 to $125; large from $150 to $250. Cleaning of the filters is usually included.

- *Supermarket carts.* $.50 to $1.00 each. Some operators make their living just doing these if they land a contract with a chain of supermarkets.

Profitable Add-Ons

New Construction Clean-Up. This usually involves concrete cleaning, curbing, pillars, parking lots, etc. Pricing can be based on those listed above. But there can be such a variety of work, you may want to consider how long it will take and use your hourly rate.

Graffiti. This too is varied. You may wish to quote your hourly rate in the beginning until you know what you are doing. Your janitorial supplier can help you with the appropriate chemicals. Be safety conscious and watch the overspray or your insurance may need to buy new paint jobs for all the cars in the area.

Final Tips

Caution! Be careful about too much pressure on some surfaces and check your local regulations on wastewater. If there are strict wastewater restrictions in your area, you may need to use a more sophisticated system that disposes of or recycles the waste. As for additional chemicals and acids, occasionally you may need to use some. Your equipment supplier will often be a big help as to what to use.

Also be aware that preventive maintenance is very critical on this type of equipment. While these machines are sturdy, neglect will quickly bring on problems, causing you the added expense of repair or replacement. You will want to keep a log, such as the one in Figure 32.1. Be sure you and anyone else using your machine keeps a detailed log or you will pay dearly in repair costs as well as lost business during down time. You will also want to be very safety conscious when using this equipment. Pointed at a foot or a person, 4,000 psi of water can be deadly. In addition to the log, Figure 32.2 illustrates an instruction and safety sheet my company requires all our operators to strictly follow. If you follow each safety procedure closely, you and your insurance company will appreciate it. Keep a copy of instructions for your pressure washer next to your machine at *all* times. Skipping *one* detail can result in damage to the unit.

The new turbo heads on the end of the wand are a great improvement. They will increase your production time on horizontal surfaces two to four times. The cost will run about $100 to $125. There is also a device that looks like a lawn mower that attaches to the end of your wand called a rotating-surface cleaner. The cost is $500 to $1,000. That is not bad for a light-to-medium-duty concrete cleaner.

The smaller pressure washers are very compact in size and can be deceiving as to their power output. Safety is stressed so strongly in this chapter because carelessness for just an instant can cause injury. Be constantly aware of the potential to harm yourself and others around you.

You also will want to consider wearing a good wrist brace in addition to the other safety equipment. The torque on the wrist from that much water pressure can eventually cause you some problems.

To conclude this section, remember that you can get the edge over your competition following the same principles outlined in the earlier sections and chapters of this book. Be uniformed and professional and do quality work.

FIGURE 32.1: Maintenance Log

Maintenance Log							
Operator's Name	Date	Start Time	End Time	Hours Used	Oil Change	Pump Oil	Problems

FIGURE 32.2: Operating Instructions

Operating Instructions for Pressure Washer

Start-Up

1. Be sure you have read all of the owner's manual.

2. Check all connections and couplers to be sure they are secure.

3. Check oil and fluid levels (top up if necessary, but do not overfill).

4. Fill gas tank (unleaded only).

5. Connect water hose to machine.

6. *Turn on water.*

7. Squeeze gun trigger to bleed air from hose.

8. Point nozzle toward the ground or pavement securely.
   (Possibly have another person holding hose as you go to step #9.)

9. Start engine according to owner's manual.

Use

Please operate machine with safety in mind at all times.

• NEVER point the wand at anyone for ANY reason. (4,000 psi could put an eye out or even worse.)

• NEVER operate the machine if you are overtired for any reason.

• NEVER operate the machine with children within 50 feet of you. (Look up frequently to be sure no one is getting too close.)

• Do not allow anyone to operate this machine without training.

• Wear safety glasses, ear plugs, gloves, and other protective clothing.

CHAPTER
33

Restaurant Cleaning

This is a profitable specialty that helped me get established years ago. There are two subspecialties involved:

1. Kitchen area: regular maintenance and specialized hood and filter cleaning.

2. Dining and lobby areas: regular maintenance and carpet cleaning.

Although many restaurants use separate services for these two areas, you want both! This is definitely a natural add-on for a pressure washing business. In fact, you will find pricing on cleaning kitchen hoods and filters in the pressure washing section.

Who Will Use My Service

- Any restaurant, large or small

- School cafeterias

- Country clubs, civic clubhouses, private clubs — anywhere there are large kitchen facilities

What Is Involved

Kitchen. You may be asked to wipe down and sanitize work surfaces and clean and mop the floor. The kitchen hoods and filters collect grease. About every two to three months, everything surrounding them in the kitchen needs to be covered with plastic and they need to be pressure washed. Often filters are removed and cleaned outside. Fire regulations in many areas require restaurants to have this done, so you are providing a very necessary and potentially life-saving service.

Dining room. You will be vacuuming or spray buffing, dust mopping or sweeping floors, and depending on what the customer wants, providing normal janitorial services.

Sales Manual

Make one up and include pictures of the fronts of restaurants you clean.

Insurance

Start with liability and bonding; add others as you grow.

Equipment and Supplies

Get the same equipment you would normally use in a janitorial, as well as pressure washing, service. If carpet cleaning is frequent enough to merit buying a machine, you may wish to do so; otherwise consider renting as needed.

Pricing

If you are doing the entire job, it may mean a five- to seven-day per week contract. It will be necessary to go in late at night after the kitchen is closed or very early in the morning. You will be required to scrub mop (see Figure 28.4, How to Mop). Also clean sinks, grills, and all stainless steel. Because of the level of cleaning necessary, you will need to charge your maximum square-foot price for this area. (Five-day is four to six cents per square foot per week).

Pricing for hood-cleaning service:

- Small hoods: $100 to $125 (filters included).
- Large hoods: $150 to $250 (filters included).

It takes two people about two-and-a-half hours to clean the exhaust hoods at the average restaurant that has three hoods. The bill would be around $350 for this alone. However, the Japanese steak houses have a grill and hood at each table, with the chef entertaining the guests while preparing their meal in front of them. Thus, there is a beautiful opportunity for a volume market here. In order to maintain a good appearance for their customers, some require this hood-cleaning service *weekly*. In such a case you could clean a dozen or so hoods and filters each week for as low as $500 and still produce an excellent profit. In some states you will have to become licensed by the health department to perform this service.

Price your dining room work at four to five cents per square foot per five-day week, plus windows (see window cleaning chapter).

Final Tips

In this specialty, $15,000 to $25,000 a year contracts are not unusual. Also, when the restaurant is carpeted, the carpet is subjected to a lot of spilled food, which is also tracked and crushed into the carpet. A good restaurant that has, for example, 5,000 square feet of carpet should get it cleaned at least twice per month. A bid of, 15 cents per square foot will be a nice addition of $1,500 per month or $18,000 per year. So by being alert to this add-on, you could easily double the value of an account per year.

It is good, hard work, but, in addition to the money, there may be another hidden benefit. Some restaurant owners may have the cooks leave you a delicious gourmet goodie (leftover from that night's special). Bon Appétit!

Restroom Service

What is a restroom specialist? A toilet jockey? A potty person? No! None of these silly or degrading titles apply. The successful restroom specialist is in reality a microbiology specialist. That person is making as much money per hour as the vice-president that runs your local bank, possibly more. This is one of the hottest rapid-growth service industries you will find. Start-up costs are so low that a person on unemployment could start one and get out of that unemployment line for good.

Why the fancy name — microbiology specialist? Simple. Restrooms are germ centers, and therefore you'd better know what you are doing when you clean them.

Pathogenic microorganisms — those that can cause disease or death — can flourish easily in a restroom. Bacteria left by bodily fluids, can double in 15 minutes. Even if the previous user of a toilet was neat and careful (which is rare), when the toilet is flushed, a very fine mist of water that could contain contagious fecal bacteria rises and falls on the toilet seats and flush handles. These germs are tough survivors. The only solution is a well-kept, properly disinfected restroom. This applies to flush valves, water faucets, push plates, sinks, toilets, and urinals, as well as floors.

What Is Involved

The franchises that specialize in this service have experienced phenomenal growth. They have mastered the basics and so can you. In order to be good at this specialty, you must:

- Thoroughly clean the restroom
- Properly disinfect
- Be fast

Number three is important if you want to make $30 to $50 per hour at this. You will want to read one of the books on speed cleaning as recommended under the section about maid services. Then clean each restroom yourself in the beginning as you develop time standards. Require future employees to meet these standards.

When you first get an account, the work will be extensive. A job that could normally take 15 to 30 minutes might take a few hours. For example, the first time you clean a restroom, you will need to remove deposits that have collected under the lip of the toilet or urinal. Prepare for that and price accordingly. You will want to develop time and price standards for both situations.

When you make your initial sales call, take the prospect into the restroom to one of the toilets. Using a hand mirror, show this germ city to him or her. Share some facts about the pathogenic microorganisms. That will probably be enough to convince anyone. You might then ask if he or she ever uses that restroom. If so, you've probably made a sale, both for the initial clean-up and the regular service.

Sales Manual

You will want to prepare a nice-looking sales manual. Include the latest information (in simplified form) on pathogenic microorganisms and OSHA's blood-pathogens requirements. Also include step-by-step photographs of you or an employee cleaning the various critical areas in a restroom (a nice touch.)

Insurance

You will need liability and bonding and other employee-related insurances as you hire.

Equipment and Supplies

You can start with as little as $100 or $200 and operate out of the trunk of your car. You will need normal restroom cleaning supplies and basic equipment (brushes, mops, etc.). Your janitorial supplier will help. Be sure to include a pumice stick in your cart or supply belt for those stubborn spots in the toilet bowl. The following items will be needed as well:

- Glass cleaner
- Disinfectant toilet cleaner
- Disinfectant surface cleaner
- Stainless steel cleaner
- Disinfectant floor cleaner concentrate
- Toilet mops and brushes
- Disposable cleaning towels
- Mop bucket and wringer
- Grout cleaning brush

The customer is expected to provide the toilet paper, paper towels, liquid soap, seat covers, trashcan liners, etc.

As with all the other service businesses, appearance is very important. Always take pride in your personal appearance even though this is dirty work. You and your workers should always wear uniform shirts, smocks, or aprons on the job. The professional appearance is well worth the investment.

Also, don't skimp on protective wear. Don't even think of cleaning a restroom without protection for yourself and your workers. Protective goggles and rubber gloves are a must if you don't want to go home after a hard day's work with some invisible guests.

Pricing

You will want to make up a comprehensive price list. Include a copy on the last page of your sales manual. Develop it the same way we recommended for many of the other service businesses. Do it yourself, time it, and then price it.

Some of the successful franchises in this specialty price per fixture, plus add-ons or options. It is simple for you to develop such a system as well if you follow the above recommendation. For example: price $1.50 to $3.00 per toilet or urinal.

Your customers really need your service every day. But most won't pay for that. For a disinfectant program to be effective it should be done daily or even twice per day. Most customers will only pay for this service once per week. Some will buy up to three times per week and then have one of their own employees check it between your visits. Using the workloading system to price, you will adjust your pricing, depending on the number of times the customer wants complete service and whether you will be making checkup visits in between.

Profitable Add-Ons

Air freshening systems can provide an additional source of income. There are two types available, dormant and motor-operated. Check on current prices from your supplier and then add on your profit for providing the service.

Final Tips

Work from the top down — mirrors and stall tops, then sinks, toilets, and urinals. Disposable gloves are a necessity. Be sure you have all the paper supplies you will need with you before you come. Work in a circle. Empty trash. Inspect and then mop or sweep yourself out the door.

If you pursue this specialty of cleaning, you will want to keep up-to-date with the industry standards. New and more resistant bacteria come on the scene constantly. Begin educating yourself and make your education ongoing. Become a true expert in your field. The trade journals and OSHA can help you with this.

Don't underestimate the potential of this humble business. It is tremendous!

Security Guard Service

Crime statistics show this time-honored profession is needed more than ever. This service fills a special need. True, electronic surveillance systems have put a dent in demand, but they cannot take the place of human oversight. Actually, the human security guard very much appreciates the help of the new electronic eyes that help the guard do a superior job.

This industry provides a wonderful opportunity for older or retired people. Many retired people who were in law enforcement have the opportunity to put their skills to good use. Even my grandfather (a retired vaudeville comedian) worked in this field until he could not work anymore.

Who Will Use My Service

- Banks
- Factories
- Warehouses
- Office buildings

- Private communities or apartment buildings
- Marinas
- Individuals or homeowners

What Is Involved

When you see a large office complex with security guards patrolling the halls and perimeters of the buildings, you are often observing an outside service contracted by the building owners. Often two shifts are required, but some companies will even contract with you for a light-duty daytime shift. (Employee theft costs billions of dollars every year.)

In most cases, you and your employees' neatly uniformed presence and a dignified and professional conduct serve as an effective crime deterrent.

Sales Manual

A sales manual is a definite must, including pictures of you and your staff in uniform. Uniforms can be purchased or rented from a security uniform service. Also, your sales manual should include your references and a copy of your bonding insurance.

Insurance

You will need bonding and liability, of course. But this labor-intensive business will also require you to have employee-related insurance coverages.

Equipment and Supplies

This gets into an area of personal preferences. I would prefer a well-trained German shepherd at my side, rather than a .357 magnum. But your main equipment will be uniforms and two-way radios. Neither the customer whose premises you are guarding nor law-enforcement agencies want you to go around shooting people. In most cases, you are hired as a watchful observer who would immediately report a break-in or any trouble to the police.

Pricing

You will need to bid on a few contracts in order to see what your local competition is getting. But generally price your work by eight-hour shifts. Some bid as low as $20 per hour to as high as $60 per hour — depending on the area, the shifts required, and the risk.

Profitable Add-Ons

How about adding on a courier service for your clients? Perhaps the company's top executives would desire a personal security guard to travel with them. Another suggestion might be to add a chauffeur or limousine service.

With regard to work in private homes, security systems are hot and you may be able to expand into this area. House-sitting services are also catching on.

Final Tips

As to the training required, find a training program near you by contacting the International Association of Professional Security Consultants (see reference in the Appendix). The training is short-term. If you use guard dogs, shop carefully for well-trained animals. Also research the lineage or background of the animals' parents. Look for an animal that is not only well-trained, but has a solid temperament, is controllable, and is not a danger to children.

Don't be intimidated in the beginning about bidding on large profitable jobs. A 250,000-square-foot facility might require a staff of only four to six people (working two shifts). The client will tell you in most cases exactly how many people he or she wants. Also, market your service to high-security apartment houses and upscale gated communities. If your service involves patrolling in vehicles, add in that cost to the prices already discussed. If you include a guard dog or dogs with your service, then you must price them by the hour and add that on, too. However, if you are pricing at the upper end of the per hour scale, you could afford to include a dog per person a great selling point.

Smoke and Fire Restoration

This in my opinion is one of the most profitable of all the service businesses. Some office cleaning companies have diversified into this field. My company did, but after doing it for ten years, I can honestly say it is better to run this business separately. It will, however, complement a carpet cleaning or water damage restoration operation.

Who Will Use My Service

You will be working for property owners who have sustained damage from fire or smoke. However, most of your business will be as a result of referrals from insurance agents and adjusters. For that reason, you will no doubt start out by calling on insurance agencies in your area. Start with you own insurance agency — you've got a foot in the door there.

What Is Involved

You will go in and clean a house or business that has smoke damage from a kitchen, furnace, chimney, or other fire. Sometimes it was not a fire that caused structural damage, but merely a furnace backfire that sent smoke through the home's vents and put a layer of soot on everything. In some cases you will be responsible to subcontract or arrange for carpentry, painting, electrical, plumbing, and even cabinet and furniture refinishing. Dry cleaning of draperies and clothes is also subcontracted.

You will be working with three different people: the insurance agency manager, the insurance adjuster, and the homeowner. This will require good people skills. Often the homeowner will want more from you than the insurance is willing to cover. This is fine if the homeowner is willing to pay for it out of pocket, but that is seldom the case. You will have to keep the insurance adjuster and/or agency manager well informed. It is easy to be caught in the middle of a dispute, and that's where diplomacy comes in. Of course, that is how you earn the profits available in this business.

Sales Manual

Bring it with you to show the homeowner on the initial call. It can also be used to impress insurance adjusters and agency managers. Besides your references, it should include before and after pictures of jobs you have already done.

Insurance

You will need liability and bonding and employee-related insurances when you hire help.

Equipment and Supplies

This is a specialized field. It requires special supplies. Most janitorial supply houses will not stock what you will need. Therefore, you will need to locate a supplier carrying and producing the unique products for this specialty.

Such suppliers will often have a wealth of information in the form of videos and booklets. I don't normally mention a supplier by name of this book, but suppliers in this field are hard to find. Chemspec in Baltimore, Maryland, has maintained an impressive reputation for the quality of their management and products for the specialty.

Some of the supplies you will need are as follows:

- *Chemical sponges*. These are dry sponges that clean smoke off walls and ceilings. (If you run short and are in a bind for these, discount stores are now selling them individually.) There is also a liquid that can be sprayed on to remove these stains.

- *Wall cleaner.* Usually sold in powder form.

- *Deodorizer chemicals.*

- *Special wood cleaner and polish.*

- *General purpose cleaners.* These are the same as you would use in home or office cleaning.

- *Carpet cleaning equipment.* See chapter on carpet cleaning.

- *Painting equipment.* Unless you subcontract it out. See chapter on painting.

Pricing

Figure 36.1 is a comprehensive price list. Feel free to use it as a guide. However, as with all pricing in this book, test the market in your part of the country first. See what others are getting and then adjust your prices accordingly. The most successful price on the high end of the scale and do work that is worthy of your price.

Depending on the level of smoke damage in a structure, three or four good workers can clean up a moderate three-bedroom house (approximately 1,200 to 1,400 square feet) in one-and-a-half to two days. For a business, using this gauge of square footage, you can pretty well estimate how long it will take your crew. Much of what needs to be done is just old-fashioned cleaning. The homeowners usually benefit in that, unless they are meticulous housekeepers, you take care of their next spring cleaning. The bill is usually $1,500 to $2,500 for just the cleaning. Dry cleaning, painting, and other options listed below can increase the bill substantially.

Profitable Add-Ons

Dry cleaning. Regarding the dry cleaning, you would charge to remove, transport to dry cleaners, and re-hang drapes. If any clothes closets were smoked up, you will also take clothing to be cleaned. Shop for a good, skilled dry cleaner. You will be providing quite a volume of business (in some cases, a truckload of drapery and clothing). Therefore, you will want a dry cleaner who offers a commission of 20 to 30 percent. This is standard in many areas.

Painting. Painting is also another profitable add-on. However, if you do this yourself rather than subcontract, be sure you or an employee is a professional. No matter how hard you worked to clean, it is the painter who will make the job appear good or bad.

FIGURE 36.1: Suggested Pricing for Smoke and Fire Restoration

Suggested Pricing for Smoke and Fire Restoration

Wall and ceiling wash. . . . . 9 cents sq. ft./up
Dry sponge . . . . 9 cents sq. ft./up
Textured ceilings . . . . 14 cents sq. ft./up
Wood & other uncarpeted floor, damp mopping . . . . 8 cents sq. ft./up
Wood & other uncarpeted floor, stripping . . . . 18 cents sq. ft./up
Wood & other uncarpeted floor, waxing. . . . . 12 cents sq. ft./up
Carpet cleaning . . . . 20 cents sq. ft./up
Rooms with very minor smoke or soot damage:
(Walls and ceilings chemically dusted, carpet vacuumed;
Horizontal surfaces dusted) average-size room. . . . . $15 to $20
Bathrooms: Full size $35/up
              Half size $25/up
Kitchen appliances: refrigerator, range, etc $4/up
Closets: walls, ceilings, and floors $15/up
Upholstered chairs: Small $12/up
                       Medium $14/up
                       Large $16/up
                       Ottoman. $6/up
Upholstered sofas: W/O skirts or removable cushions . . . . $5.50/run.ft.
                      W/O skirt, W/removable cushions . . . . $6/run.ft.
                      W/Skirt & removable cushions. $6.50/run.ft.
                      Velvet . . . . Add $2.50/run.ft.
Collections, knick-knacks, dishes, and other contents priced per job.
Dining chairs. $2.50-3.50
Dining table. $6/up
Pictures & paintings: Small $1.50/up
                         Medium $2/up
                         Large $2.50/up
Small, non-ornate lamp and shade. $2
Non-ornate floor lamp and shade $2.50
Dresser or chest up to triple (inside and out) $6-20
Cupboards and contents $30/up
Interior painting: 1 Coat . . . . 12 cents sq.ft.+ Paint
                      2 Coats . . . . 18 cents sq.ft.+ Paint
Exterior painting:. . . . . Add 20% to above
Estimates prepared for claim settlements $25/up

SMOKE ODOR REMOVAL:

| Sq.Ft. | Smoke Odor Level | | |
	Light	Medium	Heavy
1,000	$ 56	$ 72	$ 80
2,000	86	104	124
3,000	122	150	178

Duct cleaning and sealing. Another profitable add-on service. Or you may sub-contract this, if you are not set up for it.

Odor removal. Another profitable add-on. You may go with one or a combination of professional chemical aerosols and ozone machines (watch your local codes) for this purpose.

Final Tips

If you comfort the frustrated and scared homeowner after the fire, word will get around.

If you maintain impeccable honesty in your dealings with the homeowner, the insurance agency, and adjuster, word will get around.

If you go back immediately if the customer calls about an area you missed, word will get around.

And, believe me, when that word gets around, you will have all the work you can stand.

Caution! In spite of doing everything honestly and correctly, you may occasionally run into a problem collecting your money. You see, the insurance company pays the homeowner, who in turn should pay you. Shortly after doing a first-rate job on a house, my check was delivered to the homeowner. The homeowner used the insurance money to finance a nice vacation in Florida and it took months and a lot of phone calls to finally get my money. Learning my lesson, immediately after that I developed a work authorization and direct payment request form (see Figure 36.2). *Before* we start a job we require every homeowner to sign it.

In spite of the problems and challenges, if you can keep your cool and use diplomacy, you will find this an exciting and very rewarding business.

FIGURE 36.2: Work Authorization and Direct Payment Request

Work Authorization and Direct Payment Request

I authorize _____ to perform the following work: _____, in accordance with my insurance company, _____.

I understand that my property, which has been damaged, will be restored to the state it was just prior to the accident, within reason.

I also authorize my insurance company to make direct payment to _____ _____ for doing this work, and request that their name be included on any check or draft issued consequent to this insurance claim. I agree to pay _____ (if applicable) the amount of $_____, a deductible as outlined in my insurance policy, on or before the onset of this work.

Signed: _____

Date: _____

Use a form similar to this when you agree with the property owner on the work to be done. This will give you added assurance you will be paid for your services.

Stone Cleaning

This is a rare opportunity with minimum competition. Stone, marble, and terrazzo are found everywhere and yet few know how to maintain or restore them. To be specific, there is a lot of competition in major cities, but minimum or no competition in most small- to medium-sized cities. In fact, in many of these locations the market is wide open.

What has made this a volume business opportunity is the fact that in the early to mid-1980s the technology to make marble tile (instead of slabs) was developed. So in the 1980s billions of square feet of this tile was sold and installed. Now this tile is ready for professional restoration and maintenance, but very few people know what to do with it. That's where you come in.

Who Will Use My Service

- Banks

- Office buildings

- Schools

- Homes
- Anywhere you find marble floors

What Is Involved

The day-to-day maintenance of these products is not very complicated and can easily be learned. The market for you is the restoration to a new look for these products. For a marble floor, as an example, this involves going in and grinding and polishing the floor to a showroom shine. That is pretty well the key to a lot of this work: grind and polish using the right equipment; then maintain it with the proper chemicals and finishes.

Some training, however, is involved. A number of major suppliers of these products conduct seminars around the country (see Appendix). There are also some good videos available, plus a series of books.

Sales Manual

Be sure to include the standard items — proposal or agreement and before and after pictures.

Insurance

You will need liability and bonding.

Equipment and Supplies

Grinders, polishers, and compounds will set you back $6,000 to $9,000 for small- to medium-size jobs as you start out. Ultimately, as you get very large jobs, you will have $30,000 or so invested. A listing of an outstanding supplier of the equipment and supplies, as well as training seminars, is in the Appendix.

Pricing

This is the best part of learning this. Prices vary from as high as $25 per square foot in New York to as low as a few dollars per square foot in Miami, Florida. But remember, we are encouraging you to go after the market in small to medium cities and metropolitan areas. The average price across the country for restoring a marble floor is about $5 to $6 per square foot. Cost of material is around 20 cents per square foot. A good operator can do an area of about 300 square feet per day. At $6 per square foot, that's $1,800 per day! At the end of a full day's work like this, have your chauffeur pick you up and drive you home.

Profitable Add-Ons

- Floor maintenance
- Concrete cleaning and sealing

Final Tips

This is a service that is essentially in its infancy. Now is the time to carve out your place in this field. It is like a major hamburger chain was 30 years ago. Those who get in on it now and succeed will do exceptionally well. The franchises are already jumping on it. But you can get in on the ground floor without the franchise fees by contacting the people recommended. Using the business principles outlined in the first part of this book, you have a great opportunity.

CHAPTER 38

Swimming Pool Service

As the cost of installing a swimming pool has become more in the reach of the average household, a swimming pool maintenance service becomes more in demand. This industry has evolved in recent years. Technology has greatly simplified the chemical maintenance for a pool so that the average pool owner can easily test the water. However, most would rather not bother, plus there is the task of keeping it clean — that's where you come in. Whether the pool is in a residence or is public, most would rather not keep up with this responsibility if they could get it done reasonably. It is one of the more respected and profitable of the traditional service businesses.

Who Will Use My Service

- You have a potential customer anywhere you find a swimming pool.
- Private homes
- Hotels/motels
- Condominiums and developments with community pools
- Health clubs

What Is Involved

Annually. Replacing the hydrostatic relief valve (from the main drain pump) runs $40 to $50. This valve costs you around $20. Clean pool thoroughly. Acid wash or paint (or both) — price depends on size. Flush out chemicals. Balance the pH to about 6.8 of the total alkalinity to 60 parts per million. Add chlorine until it reaches 2.0 PPM, and then shock the pool to 10 PPM.

Monthly or Weekly. Check and adjust the balance of chemicals in the pool and then give it a good cleaning. The weekly and monthly business is what you want to promote. It is the bread and butter of this business. Heavily used resort pools will require more — perhaps daily service.

Sales Manual

Not necessary.

Insurance

Liability is sufficient.

Equipment and Supplies

Floating cleaners, test kits, skimmers, and chemicals. Total start-up costs can be less than $1,000.

Pricing

A regular service route, when built up, can produce $50 an hour. A 20- by 40-foot residential pool will average $125 a month for weekly service. However, the same size pool with greater use, such as a motel, will average $300 to $400 a month for service five or six times a week. Options like as seasonal work — pool painting and repair — should be billed using the workloading system discussed earlier.

Profitable Add-Ons

- Landscaping
- Housesitting and home security
- Pool installation and sales

Also, a new specialty that has surfaced in the last few years is leak detection and repair service for pools. Investigate it with your local pool and spa dealers. It's hot!

Final Tips

Spas are big in this market. Their growth among homeowners is amazing. Go after this market, as the spa owner soon tires of keeping up with the unique chemistry a spa must maintain. Use the pricing principles we have outlined. Talk to the large spa and pool suppliers in your area. See if they can be of help by providing some leads or letting you leave a supply of your cards. Also, send out discount or free check-up flyers in the mail to the more affluent neighborhoods.

The full-time market for this service seems to be south of the border, but pools and particularly spas are everywhere. Jump in!

Temporary Help Service

More than ever businesses are turning to temporary (or temp) services. Their employee-related costs keep going up, and they have seen the wisdom of using a temporary worker rather than hiring for certain jobs. This is a labor-intensive business for you the provider, but the benefits make it worthwhile.

Who Will Use My Service

- All types of businesses
- Out of town businesses with a temporary job in your area
- Factories needing temporary clean-up help during shutdowns

What Is Involved

You will need to have good organizational skills. This business could be started in your home and later expanded to a rented office in the business district.

Finding good help will be your first priority. You probably already know some people who could be called on. They may not want to work full time, but may enjoy keeping their skills current on a part-time basis. Then more help can be obtained by advertising in the classified section of newspapers. Another source — contact local schools, colleges, and technical schools.

Have some business cards printed. Next you may wish to use the targeting approach to contact businesses most likely to use your service. Advertise in the telephone book, local newspapers, and possibly on cable TV. You may wish to join the chamber of commerce and attend some meetings of business people in your community in order to make contacts.

Sales Manual

Your sales manual should be given considerable thought and planning. While it should not be too lengthy, this invaluable tool will show potential clients the type of people you have and help them see through numerous pictures and illustrations how you can help them through a particularly busy time or an outbreak of the flu. Confidence is a must in this business. Your presentation can go a long way in instilling faith in you and your people.

Insurance

As mentioned earlier, this is a labor-intensive business. Therefore, a number of the following insurances may be needed:

- Liability
- Bonding
- Unemployment
- Workers' compensation
- Health care (possibly)

Equipment and Supplies

You could start from a home-based office for as little as $2,000 to $3,000. This would include:

- A computer with billing and payroll software
- Ink-jet or laser printer
- Telephone answering machine or service
- Fax machine
- Basic office supplies

You will also want to have funds available to meet payroll costs as you get started.

Pricing

Pricing will require a knowledge of the normal local salaries for the positions you will be filling. The trade standard markup for temporary services is about 50 percent — higher for professional temporaries and lower for less skilled workers.

Profitable Add-Ons

Depending on the help you are able to secure, you can offer the following:

- Temporary maids, cooks, etc. for parties
- Nannies and baby sitters
- Daycare workers
- Secretarial services
- Computer programmers
- Videographers to video events
- Pet/plant/house sitters

Final Tips

You will no doubt start small. Concentrate on hiring the best people you can. If you don't know a person well, check references carefully. Don't assume they know the job — train them and implement an ongoing training program even if the fill-in jobs are considered menial, then target the prime accounts to fit your employees' abilities.

However, you will find this business has the potential to grow rapidly. Before this happens, have everything in place; consult with a good accountant, lawyer, insurance agent, and tax expert. The stress such growth will add can be minimized by preplanning, and the increased profits (average $20,000 to $80,000) will make it worth while.

Trash Removal

I first got interested in this business when I found my company could pick up a few hundred dollars simply by hauling off the ruined items from a home owner after a fire or flood. Then I noticed that the trash removal service that picked up at my home started out using an old one-ton truck with a wood bed, but now was driving new high-tech trash trucks that cost as much as a new house. As time went on, I moved to an upscale plantation development on the coast. Now my trash service not only drives a high-tech trash truck that costs as much as a house, but the owner dresses and looks like an ivy-league executive and lives in the same development.

Have the majority of us so-called professionals been missing something? I suspect so. There's money in garbage.

Consider: the average hospital is spending around $75,000 a year for trash removal; the average college about $55,000; the average school about $31,000. Did you know that some large national companies are buying out the small operators in an effort to dominate this market? But there is still an excellent opportunity in most areas for a modest-sized operation.

Who Will Use My Service

- Homes and businesses

What Is Involved

A weekly or biweekly service is provided to pick up your customer's trash. You will then deposit it at the local designated dump or landfill. Usually a per-load or weight fee is involved. Also, more and more communities are enforcing ecological regulations for trash disposal. Because costs are rising, many services limit a customer to two cans with liners or two bags. Plus they require the customer to leave their trash containers at the curb. However, many still desire pull-in service and are willing to pay the extra for it.

Even more profitable is the commercial business. If you can obtain a route of regular business customers, it will mean fewer stops. However, you will need a truck with the lifts to handle dumpsters.

Due to the profit involved, it may be difficult to secure the more profitable routes at first. Therefore, starting small with a minimal investment will help you stay in the black while you build your customer base.

Sales Manual

Not necessary.

Insurance

Get liability and vehicle insurance. Employee-related insurance will be needed as you grow.

Equipment and Supplies

Start small, perhaps with a one- or two-ton used truck with a dump bed. The cost is $5,000 to $15,000 or more. Once you establish a nice route, it will pay you to invest in a good quality garbage truck. If you have a good route, you won't sweat the payments. A new rear-loader truck costs around $120,000 and a new front-loader truck, around $180,000.

Pricing

Prices vary greatly in various areas of the country. Residential, once-per-week service seems to do well for $125 to $150 per year per customer. A twice per week service does well at $180 to $250 per year. Some bill monthly, others quarterly.

Commercial loads usually must be priced based on weight and type of refuse. Then you will need to figure in the landfill charges that you will have to pay.

Profitable Add-Ons

Recycling. In some areas there are recycling centers that will retrieve recyclable items from your load, or some have done this themselves, adding to profit with the sale of recyclable items. Encouraging customers to separate recyclable items in separate bags for pick up will save much work — and many people are glad to do it.

Profitable add-ons include brush and leaf removal at $100 to $150 per one-ton truckload. High volume dumpster service is a specialty in itself. Once you establish a residential service, investigate this possibility. It's awesome!

Final Tips

If you do good work and leave the curb clean of any fallen trash and you put the empty cans back neatly, you will do well. In the beginning, go house to house in your uniform and ask for the business (or use the phone, but that's not as effective). Leave a business card at each house.

After a few years of operation, I sincerely hope you enjoy your two-week cruise to Hawaii.

Tree Trimming

This is a profitable specialty that has equal application as a full-time business or an excellent part-time job. It will surprise you how much you can make in this business. This is true whether you run a small operation with a few chain saws, a ladder, and a pickup truck or an advanced operation using bucket extension trucks and commercial shredders.

Who Will Use My Service

- Homeowners
- Land developers
- Condominium and development associations
- Business property owners
- Insurance agencies

What Is Involved

Most of the work involves the removal of trees and limbs that are diseased, damaged, or just in the way of a construction project. You may find yourself involved in high-volume work if you live in a tornado or hurricane prone area. Fortunes are made in a matter of months in such areas after a bad storm. As in the case of other disaster restoration services, this is a needed, respected, and high profitable specialty.

Sales Manual

You don't need a full-blown sales manual, but a list of references is good to have.

Insurance

Liability and vehicle insurance are all you should need.

Equipment and Supplies

Your equipment needs depend on how far you want to get into this service.

For a part-timer or college student working through school, a used pickup truck ($1,000 to $5,000), a couple of good chain saws ($200 to $300 each) with an extendible unit (another $100), extension ladders ($100 to $500) and other gear — climbing belt, goggles, safety hat, etc. ($100+) are enough.

For the operator who wants to advance in this business, add to the above a bucket truck, used or new for $25,000 to $125,000.

Pricing

As a general rule, a good tree trimmer is worth $50 to $75 per hour in many areas. Storms will produce big profits, but you have to eat between them. So contract apartment or business complexes for tree trimming. In such a case, you would automatically check and trim their trees monthly or seasonally (four times a year). You will charge the high end of the scale when you use a bucket truck. This is because you get more done in an hour — and you have to pay for the thing.

During special storm clean-up work that will require overnight travel, you will charge your hourly rate plus expenses (food, motel, mileage). However, since price gouging is common at such times, you must use good judgment and price fairly, letting the volume provide your profit.

Profitable Add-Ons

- Landscaping service
- Mulch sales

Final Tips

The main thing you need in this business is a lot of common sense. You constantly need to be very safety conscious. A bad fall or a brush with a power line can put you out of business or worse.

Perhaps working with an upscale service would help you learn the ropes before breaking out on your own. For example, unless you have horticultural training, you will need to learn the times of the year the sap runs in the trees, where and how to make cuts on a tree so as not to damage or kill it, etc. A community college library can be helpful.

CHAPTER 42

Water Damage Restoration

Although I would normally recommend this business as a diversification for a smoke and fire restoration service or a carpet cleaning business, in a number of areas of the country this business can stand on its own feet. With climate changes, more and more areas are seeing flood and water damage than ever before. In a sense this is very unfortunate for many a customer in a flood zone, but an honest operator will quickly build a good business with insurance companies in these areas. Plus you will provide a desperately needed service.

Who Will Use My Service

Home and business owners, but you will find much of your business will come through referrals by insurance agents.

What Is Involved

You will be expected by the owner and/or insurance company to remove water from a home or business resulting from a broken water pipe, a leaky roof, storm damage, or a flood.

Carpeting and other items will need to be thoroughly dried. If possible, you will be expected to clean the carpet and furniture. If anything is ruined, you may also be contracted to remove and dispose of it. Is the sheetrock damaged? After tearing it out, sound framing will still require time to dry out before sealing with new sheet rock or paneling. Insulation may be affected as well and need replacing. Replacement of the walls may also call for painting and wallpapering. What about electrical wiring? Often the insurance company asks you to oversee all of this and you may have to subcontract things such as electrical work. Or perhaps you have been subcontracted just to do the water damage clean up. Finally, you will be expected to deodorize.

Sales Manual

One is definitely needed, especially to impress insurance agencies and adjusters before the need arises. Include references, pictures of some of your major equipment, and before and after pictures.

Insurance

Get liability, bonding, and employee-related insurance as needed.

Equipment and Supplies

Although you can get away with using portable carpet cleaning machines on smaller jobs, you will need the following:

- A good truck-mount unit for the large jobs. Cost for this varies from $6,000 to $15,000 or more new to $2,500 to $5,000 for used.

- One or more ozone generators (for odor), which run $500 to $1,000 each.

- Thermal foggers, fans, blowers, dehumidifiers and desiccant drying machines (to remove moisture from walls and floors), ultrasonic cleaning machine, water pump, generator, and possibly a sump pump and flood suckers.

You may start out for a few thousand, but all of these items will eventually be in your budget if you go into this in a major way. You could easily in time have $100,000 or more in your equipment. However, the first big flood may pay it all off, plus buy you a new truck.

Additionally, there are some basic supplies listed in the chapter for smoke and fire restoration that you will use, with the exception of chemical sponges.

Pricing

Much of our smoke and fire price list will help you arrive at some of the prices. However, due to the nature of this work when it is done on a major scale, you may wish to provide your equipment (ozone machines or dehumidifiers) on a rental fee per job and price some of your work by the hour. A cooperative adjuster and insurance agency can help you fine-tune these figures with fair pricing in your area. Also to be considered, when disaster strikes, sheer volume will provide your profit. Charging top dollar at such times will earn you a bad reputation.

Profitable Add-Ons

Droughts do happen, and broken water pipes are somewhat rare. So adding smoke and fire restoration and/or carpet cleaning services will keep you busy. They require much of the same equipment.

Final Tips

Early in your business, collect a pool of temporary help to call on during a disaster or emergency. Offer them twice their regular wage, making it worth their time to come and help you.

Before undertaking the investment of this type of specialty, I recommend you go to one of the two- to five-day training seminars for this field (see Appendix).

43

Window Cleaning

This is one of the easiest of all the service businesses to start. It also involves one of the lowest equipment and supply investments ($100 to $200). However, there is plenty of competition, and this scares off a lot of people. As has been said many times so far, for this and all other service businesses, if an operator looks sharp and does neat work, the chances for success are great.

This is an excellent part-time business for students and for anyone needing extra income. It will also add-on nicely to janitorial and most home cleaning services. A nice plus too is that it is primarily a cash business. That eliminates a lot of billing and bookkeeping, but of course, not all.

Who Will Use My Service

- Retail stores
- Chain supermarkets
- Homeowners
- Office buildings
- Anywhere there is glass

What Is Involved

Primarily, there are two types of window cleaning work: residential and commercial. When you clean windows in a residence, it will pay more per square foot, but they usually only have it done once or twice a year. Commercial work, on the other hand, will produce more square footage, plus more frequency (usually once or twice a month). Chain stores may want you to do all their stores in a district, which would involve some travel.

Insurance

You will need liability and possibly, but not necessarily, bonding.

Equipment and Supplies

Buy the best. You will find a local janitorial supplier will set you up with a basic outfit. It will include squeegees of various sizes, brush or wiper, buckets, and a holster for your belt to hold your tools, saving you from bending over so much.

Now as to window cleaning solution, this is a special subject. The janitorial supplier would like to sell you premixed cleaner — a very profitable chemical sale. However, most of the pros have their own favorite formulas. Try a number of the different homemade formulas. Most work well and will save you a bundle on window cleaner. To get you started, you may want to try the following formula:

> To a bucket of water — add one half cup of ammonia and a "squirt" of non-sudsing detergent. This makes two to three gallons at a fraction of the store-bought cleaners' price.

If the weather gets really cold — don't go home. Keep and use a supply of windshield washer solution (about $1.00 to $1.50 per gallon in a discount store.) Use it straight — it has additives to prevent freezing.

Besides the above you will need poles and some medium-sized terry towels. As you get established you may want to invest in a Tucker pole. It is a neat device for reaching two- or three-storey windows without leaving the ground. Of course, if you begin to clean windows in larger buildings, be sure to be equipped with safe scaffolding and safety harnesses.

Pricing

There is a big variance from one area to another. You must balance your price between how much you need an hour and your local competition. Here are some competitive and practical prices for many areas:

Commercial

- *Small storefront.* One or two windows on each side of entrance doors should run $8 to $10 inside and out.

- *Average-size pharmacy or shop.* This should take a half-hour to an hour. The cost is $25 inside and out.

- *Average-size grocery store.* The price to do this is $30 to $40 inside and out, taking a hour to an hour-and-a-half.

- *Large store with many panes.* For unobstructed panes, the price is $2 per pane, inside and out.

- *All stores.* For outside only, charge half the price of inside and out. Although you are making a stop for less money, the outside is usually much easier than the inside because there are fewer obstacles and water drainage is not a problem.

- *High buildings.* Increase your price in proportion to the height and risk factor.

Residential

- *Casement plus storm windows.* The whole window, all four sides, is $8 to $10 per unit.

- *Double-pane glass with removable dividers.* This is usually priced at $3 to $5 per unit.

Note: As mentioned in other sections of this book, remember the rule: The higher you must go — on a ladder or using the Tucker pole — the higher the price will go.

Profitable Add-Ons

- Window repair
- Painting

- Janitorial service
- Awning cleaning

Final Tips

As you clean windows, try this procedure: Try not to wash windows in bright sun — they will dry too quickly and leave a soap residue. Brush windows, including tape or tape residue, then scrape off. Next brush thoroughly (take care to get the edges). Rinse brush often.

As you use your squeegee, keep the trailing edge of it *dry*. (Even a faint line of water will leave streaks.) If you have streaks when finished — *do it again*.

With the towel on your pole, wipe edges and ledges. Don't get water on carpets, papers, merchandise, or anything when working inside. When finished, inspect it carefully. Don't leave a job until it is done without streaks or lines. There is a lot of competition, and doing it right will give you the edge you need. That is the key to succeeding in a good window cleaning business.

Yacht Cleaning

If you love the water and live close to the ocean or a large lake, this one's for you. First you must appreciate the potential for this service. It's tremendous!

When a person pays $250,000, or even several million dollars, for a large yacht or sailboat, they usually want it properly cared for when they are in port. If you live within a reasonable distance of a good marina, you would be well advised to look into this.

Who Will Use My Service

- Boat owners — particularly larger yachts and sailboats
- Marinas
- Boat dealers

What Is Involved

First, you will want to try to make friends with the harbormaster or manager of the marina. Leave a copy of your references and any information that will impress him or her about your service. Word-of-mouth recommendation will bring in much business. In some cases, some services offer the marina a commission for customer referrals that result in new business. But at least you may be able to leave some business cards or post advertising on a bulletin board.

After you get a customer, your work will be similar to cleaning a luxury condo. Check and be sure the power on board is compatible with your equipment. Then you will follow an organized speed cleaning procedure as explained elsewhere in this book. Be prepared, however, to know how to clean and polish a great deal of precious woods, like teak, mahogany, and cherry. Then there's the brass that needs polishing. Everything else is pretty standard.

In some cases the larger yachts have the crew to do this, but in many cases, the owners would welcome a service. Your rates and profit will be higher than regular maid service for a number of obvious reasons. Areas are usually more cramped. There is often a lot more wood cabinetry and, in some cases, it will be done only a few times per year.

Sales Manual

Follow the same format suggested for a maid service, including a price list. Use it to sell the marina manager or harbormaster and the yacht owner.

Insurance

Get liability and bondingand employee-related insurances if you hire help.

Equipment and Supplies

See the chapter for maid service for most of your supplies. However, you will need high quality polish and waxes for the exotic woods used inside. Be prepared with hand-held and canister vacuums in case you find yourself in a tight space.

Invest in a good pair of slip-resistant deck shoes. They protect you and won't damage the boat's decks.

Pricing

Interior. As with all services, this will vary with your area. You will have to check and see what the traffic will bear. However, a suggested and a fair rate for doing just the basic cleaning (no ovens, refrigerators, or detail work on exotic cabinets and furniture) would be $125 to $175 per 1,000 square feet of interior space. Set your price list up the same way as for a maid service, only include $35 to $50 per hour in the calculation. Have your options clearly priced out.

So much for the interior service. Other than swabbing the deck, some companies also offer exterior or hull cleaning (although that is not necessary, as there are companies specializing in that alone). If you want to branch out in this, you will need to be a certified scuba diver.

Exterior. Assuming you are a qualified scuba diver, you will charge $90 to $150 per hour per diver for going under and hand cleaning the hull — the darker the water, the higher the rate.

Profitable Add-Ons

An excellent related service might be condo/apartment or regular maid service.

Depending on your interest and ability, a number of the following services are needed by yacht and boat owners.

- Painting
- Wood repair and resealing
- Fiberglass repairs
- Canvas repair
- Mildew treatment

Final Tips

All the tips for professionalism in this manual will pay off (including the wearing of uniforms — perhaps with a nautical look).

In addition to calling on the marina managers, run a small ad in the newspaper that is available near the marina. Also, when you clean one for the first time, give the customer a coupon for 10 or 20 percent off the next time to encourage repeat business.

Conclusion

Now you have over 30 different service businesses to consider. They offer great opportunities. As you compare them and what to charge, you will see that it is not an exaggeration to say you can make $50 or more per hour in a service business. What is required on your part is diligence and determination, particularly when trying to secure that first account.

Since what is presented here is just an overview of suggested businesses, educate yourself as much as possible in your chosen field. The Appendix has sources of information and supplies for your use.

As you can see from the Profitable Add-On sections, many of these services are interrelated. It is easy to branch out from one to the other and increase your profit.

Are there other service businesses besides these that you could easily pursue? The list is endless. For example, you might also look into some of the following:

- Clean rooms for computers (See computer cleaning chapter)

- Duct cleaning (see home allergy proofing chapter)

- Playground equipment cleaning

- Interior plant service

- HVAC filter service

- Asphalt maintenance service

- Window blind and mini-blind cleaning

- Funeral home cleaning

- Hospital cleaning

- Snow removal

- Elevator and escalator service

- School and college cleaning

And many, many more. All require a minimum investment to get started.

The key is SERVICE. Provide the best service of your type in your area, and you will have all the work you need and the satisfaction of owning your own business. That is the essence of the message presented. Anyone with some money to invest can start a business, and many do. But the failure rate is high. Why? Most don't want to provide *service* to their customers.

Is that asking that you be married to your business? No. But it does take intelligent thinking through, planning, and organization. It's really something like show business — how you present yourself can make all the difference. Does your customer have your undivided attention when speaking to you? Do you deal with complaints with excuses or action? Does your appearance say you are proud of who you are, or do you look like something the cat dragged in?

This concept is not difficult to master, but if you do you will succeed at whatever service you provide.

Now, get out there and make some money!

Appendix

This is designed to provide sources for additional information and supplies if unavailable locally. Web sites and toll-free numbers are provided where possible.

Author's comments are in brackets — [ ].

Apartment Preparation

Supplies:

JaniSource Professional
Products Ecolab, Inc.
370 N. Wabasha St.
St. Paul, MN 55102
615-293-4108
www.janisourceproducts.com
[Most supplies can be purchased locally.]

Additional Reading:

Speed Cleaning — Jeff Cambell
Published by Dell Publishing Company, Inc.

Automobile Detailing

Supplies:

[Most supplies can be purchased locally.]

Books, Videos and Training, Equipment:

Auto Laundry News (Magazine)
2125 Center Ave., Ft. Lee, NJ 07024
201-592-7007

Professional Carwashing & Detailing (Magazine)
13 Century Hill Drive, Latham, NY 12110-1297
517-783-1281
www.carwash.com

Detailing Plus (info)
P.O. Box 20755, Portland Oregon 97294
503-251-2955, Fax 503-251-5975
e-mail: dplus@worldnet.att.net

Carwash Owners & Suppliers
Association
262-639-4393

Carpet Cleaning

Supplies, Equipment, and Training:

Argo & Company, Inc., — Argosheen
Products
170-190 Ezell St., PO Box 2747,
Spartanburg, SC 39204
864-583-9766, Fax 864-585-5056
www.argoco.com

Sun-Belt USA
4211 Atlantic Ave., Raleigh, NC 27604
800-334-8418, Fax 919-878-6518
www.sun-beltusa.com

Steam Services, Inc.
1809 N. Helm Ave. No. 5
Fresno, CA 93727
888-344-7224, Fax 559-452-9515
www.workmaster.com

Von Schrader Co.
1600 Junction Ave., Racine, WI 53403
800-626-6916, Fax 414-634-2888
www.vonschrader.com

Additional Reading:

*Carpet Cleaners Guide to Increased Sales
and Profit* — William R. Griffin
Published by Cleaning Consultant
Service, Inc.

*Building Service Contractor's Guide to
Carpet Care* — Donald E. Tepper
Published by Building Services
Contractors Assoc., International

Franchise, Training:

Steam Way International, Inc.
4550 Jackson St., Denver, CO 80216
800-447-8326 Fax 303-355-3516
www.steamway.com

Halcyon L.C. (Mfg. Hurricane Truck
Mount System)
7612 Emerald Drive
Melbourne, FL 32907
800-752-9530, Fax 407-726-9762
www.halcyonsales.com

Ceiling Cleaning and Wall Washing

Training Seminars, Manuals, Supplies, and Equipment:

ICWC
1555 Sunshine Dr.
Clearwater, FL 34625
800-628-4422

InjectiDry Systems, Inc.
P.O. Box 9644, Redmond, WA 98052
800-257-0797, Fax 425-861-1812
www.injectidry.com

Von Schrader Co.
1600 Junction Ave., Racine, WI 53403
800-626-6916, Fax 414-634-2888
www.vonschrader.com

Chimney Cleaning

Supplies:

National Chimney Supply
4219 Howard Ave.
Kensington, MD 20895
800-897-8481

RMR Products
11011 Glenoaks Blvd., #14
Pacoima, CA 91331
800-366-8677

Sand Hill Wholesale, Inc.
1955 Alum Creek Drive
Columbus, OH 43207
800-258-5496

Training:

Chimney Safety Institute of America
Indianapolis, Indiana
317-871-0030
www.ncsg.org

Computer Cleaning

Equipment and Training:

Edge Tech Industries, Inc.
7370 Opportunity Rd., Suite L
San Diego, CA 92111
800-250-2440, Fax 858-627-9130
e-mail: edgetech@ixpres.com

TECH-SA-PORT
P.O. Box 5372, Pittsburgh
PA 15206-0372
800-543-2233, Fax 412-661-3137
www.tech-sa-port.com

Concrete Cleaning and Sealing

Supplies and Training:

Ecolab, Inc. JaniSource Professional
Products
370 N. Wabasha St.
St. Paul, MN 55102
651-293-4108, Fax 651-225-3298
www.janisourceproducts.com

Hillyard, Inc.
302 N. 4th St., PO Box 909
St. Joseph, MO 64502
800-365-1555, Fax 800-861-0256
www.hillyard.com

Lincoln Service & Equipment Co.
9 Commerce Circle, Durham, CT 06473
800-349-3449, Fax 860-349-3434
www.lincolnservice.com

Spartan Chemical Co., Inc.
1110 Spartan Drive
Maumee, OH 43537
419-531-5551, Fax 419-536-8423
www.spartanchemical.com

Duct Cleaning

See Home Allergy Proofing

Floor Maintenance

Equipment, Supplies, and Training:

3M
3M Center Bldg., 223-55-07
St. Paul, MN 55144
800-852-9722, Fax 800-447-0408
www.3m.com

Alto U.S., Inc.
390 South Woods Mill Rd.
Chesterfield, MO 63017
614-205-1220, Fax 614-205-1544
e-mail: vklouse@alto-slm.com

Tornado
2501 W. Lawrence Ave.
Chicago, IL 60706
800-VACUUMS, Fax 708-867-6968
www.breuertornado.com

Graffiti Cleaning

Supplies and Training:

Alto U.S., Inc.
390 South Woods Mill Rd.
Chesterfield, MO 63017
314-205-1220, Fax 314-205-1544
e-mail: vklouse@alto-slm.com

Buckeye International, Inc.
2700 Wagner Pl.
Maryland Heights, MO 63043
800-321-2583, Fax 614-298-2850
www.buckeye-intl.com

Chemique, Inc.
315 N. Washington Ave.
Moorestown, NJ 08057
800-225-4161, Fax 856-273-0917
www.chemique.com

Hydro Tek Systems, Inc.
10418 Enterprise Drive.
Redlands, CA 92374
800-274-9376, Fax 909-799-9888
www.hydroteksystems.com

Home Allergy Proofing

Supplies and Training:

Allergy Control Products
96 Danbury Road
Ridgefield, CT 06877
203-438-9580, Fax 203-431-8963

ATI (Air Techniques, Inc.)
1717 Whitehead Rd.
Baltimore, MD 21207
Fax 410-636-9695

Bio-Tech Systems
PO Box 25380
Chicago, Illinois 60625
800-621-5545

Rowan Chemicals, Inc.
Bayside, NY 11361
800-537-6926
www.rowanchemicals.com

Duct Cleaning

American Caddy Vac, Inc.
PO Box 737
Lewiston, ID 83501
Fax 208-746-9858
www.caddyvac.com

Atlantic Engineering
11 Main St., Salisbury, MA 01952
Fax 978-462-9170
www.aeductools.com

Pringle Power Vac., Inc.
PO Box 297, Walla Walla, WA 99362
Fax 509-529-9527

SPC — Specialty Products for Cleaning
5623 Nowland Way, Arvada, CO 80002
Fax 303-424-4553

Franchise:

Ductbusters
Clearwater, FL
727-787-7087
www.ductbusters.com

Landscaping Service

Supplies:

Most supplies can be purchased locally.

Franchises:

Lawn Doctor, Inc.
800-631-5660

Spring-Green Lawn Care
800-435-4051
www.spring-green.com

NaturaLawn of America, Inc.
800-989-5444
www.nl-amer.com

Lighting Service

Supplies:

Most supplies can be purchased locally.

Professional Association:

International Association of Lighting
www.iald.org

Maid Service

Supplies:

See your local janitorial supplier.

Hillyard, Inc.
302 N. 4th St., PO Box 909
St. Joseph, MO 64502
800-365-1555, Fax 800-861-0256
www.hillyard.com

Procter & Gamble
2 Procter & Gamble Plaza
Cincinnati, OH 45202
800-332-7787

Equipment:

Oreck Corporation
100 Plantation Rd.
New Orleans, LA 70123
800-535-8810, ext. 7504
www.oreck.com

The Eureka Company
1201 East Bell St.
Bloomington, IL 61701
Fax 309-823-5442
www.eureka.com

The Hoover Co.
101 East Maple St.
North Canton, OH 44720
330-499-9200, Fax 330-966-5448
www.hoover.com

Franchises:

Maid Brigade
800-722-6243
www.maidbrigade.com

Maid To Perfection
800-648-6243
www.maidtoperfectioncorp.com

Merry Maids
800-634-7962
www.merrymaids.com

Additional Reading:

*Everything You Need To Know To Start
A House Cleaning Service* — Mary

Johnson, William R. Griffin
Published by Cleaning Consultant
Service, Inc.

Speed Cleaning — Jeff Cambell
Published by Dell Publishing Company,
Inc.

New Construction Clean-up

Supplies:

See your local janitorial supplier.

3M
3M Center Bldg., 223-55-07
St. Paul, MN 55144
800-852-9722, Fax 800-447-0408
www.3m.com

Chemique, Inc. [masonry cleaners]
315 N. Washington Ave.
Moorestown, NJ 08057
800-225-4161, Fax 856-273-0917
www.chemique.com

Clorox Professional Products Co.
1221 Broadway
Oakland, CA 94612
800-685-9128, Fax 510-271-7758
www.clorox.com

Additional Reading:

*Construction Clean-Up
For Residential Units
Construction Clean-Up* — Cleaning
Consultant Service
Published by Cleaning Consultant
Services, Inc.
206-682-9748

Office Cleaning

Supplies and Equipment:

See your local janitorial supplier.

Sun-Belt USA [Training also available]
4211 Atlantic Ave., Raleigh, NC 27604
800-334-8418, Fax 919-878-6518
www.sun-beltusa.com

Hillyard, Inc.
302 N. 4th St., PO Box 909
St. Joseph, MO 64502
800-365-1555, Fax 800-861-0256
www.hillyard.com

Franchises:

Coverall Cleaning Concepts
800-537-3371
www.coverall.com

Jani-King
800-552-5264
www.janiking.com

ServiceMaster
800-255-9687
www.svm.com

Professional Associations:

Building Service Contractors
Association International
10201 Lee Highway, Suite 225
Fairfax, VA 22030
800-368-3414

National Trade Publications/Cleaning
Management Institute
13 Century Hill Drive, Latham, NY
12110-2196
518-783-1281

Additional Reading:

Cleaning & Maintenance Management
[Magazine]
Cleanfax [Magazine]
Published by: National Trade
Publications, Inc.
13 Century Hill Drive
Latham, NY 12110-2197
www.cmmonline.com

Contracting Profits [Magazine]
Trade Press Publishing Corp
2100 W. Florist Ave.
Milwaukee, WI 53209-3799

Services [Magazine]
Building Service Contractors
Association International (BSCAI)
P.O. Box 850756
Braintree, MA 02185-9908
800-422-2681
Fax 781-848-6450

Building Services Management
(2nd Edition) — Bill Phillips
Published by MacNair-Dorland
Company, New York

Inside the Janitorial Business
Fred Massey
Published by MBM Books
PO Box 434
Encinitas, Calif. 92024

Cleaning Up For a Living
(2nd Edition)
Don Aslett & Mark Browning
Published by Betterway Books
F & W Publications, Inc.,
1507 Dana Ave.
Cincinnati, Ohio 45207

Parking Lot Cleaning

Equipment and Supplies:

Minuteman International, Inc.
111 S. Rohlwing Rd.
Addison, IL 60101
800-323-9420, Fax 630-627-1130
www.minutemaninti.com

Tymco, Inc. [Truck Models]
225 E. Industrial Blvd.
Waco, TX 76705
800-258-9626
www.tymco.com

Pest Control

Supplies:

Amrep, Inc.
990 Industrial Park Drive
Marietta, GA 30062
800-241-7766, Fax 770-422-1737
www.amrep.com

Chase Products Company
P.O. Box 70, Maywood, IL 60153
708-865-1000
www.chaseproducts.com

Cyberclean.com
6300 Lemai Ave., Chicago, IL 60646
773-775-4332
www.cyberclean.com

Noble Pine Products
P.O. Box 41, Yonkers, NY 10710-0041
800-359-4913, fax 914-664-9383
www.sterifab.com

Professional Association:

National Pest Control Association
8100 Oak Street
Dunn Loring, VA 22027

Franchises:

Terminix Termite & Pest Control
800-654-7848
www.terminix.com

Swisher Pest Control Corp.
800-444-4138
www.swisheronline.com

Pressure Washing

Equipment:

All American
7251 Varna Ave.
N. Hollywood, CA 91605
800-541-7267, Fax 818-503-8923
www.allamericanequip.com

Grainger
800-225-5994
www.grainger.com

Hydramotion
401 East Fourth St.
Bridgeport, PA 19405
800-726-1526, Fax 610-239-7863
e-mail: hydrasales@aol.com

Restaurant Cleaning

Equipment and Supplies:

See your local janitorial supplier.

3M
3M Center Bldg., 223-55-07
St. Paul, MN 55144
800-852-9722, Fax 800-447-0408
www.3m.com

All American
7251 Varna Ave.
N. Hollywood, CA 91605
800-541-7267, Fax 818-503-8923
www.allamericanequip.com

Bane-Clene Corp
3940 N. Keystone Ave.
Indianapolis, IN 46205
800-428-9512, Fax 317-543-2222
www.baneclene.com

Restroom Service

Supplies and Equipment:

See your local janitorial supplier.

Hillyard, Inc.
302 N. 4th St., PO Box 909
St. Joseph, MO 64502
800-365-1555, Fax 800-861-0256
www.hillyard.com

Kaivac, Inc.
401 S. Third St., PO Box Hamilton,
Hamilton, OH 45011

800-287-1136, Fax 513-887-4601
www.kaivac.com

Security Guard Service

See Uniforms.

International Association of
Professional Security Consultants
949-640-9918; Fax 949-640-9911
www.IAPSC.org

Smoke and Fire Restoration

Supplies and Equipment:

Chemspec
901 N. Newkirk St.
Baltimore, MD 21205
800-638-7370, Fax 800-638-6188
www.chemspecrpm.com

Steam Way International, Inc.
4550 Jackson St., Denver, CO 80216
800-447-8326, Fax 303-355-3516
www.steamway.com

Professional Association:

National Institute of Fire Restoration
4420 Fairfax Drive
Arlington, VA 22203

Additional Information:

Purofirst
800-247-9047

Steam Way International, Inc.
800-447-8326

Stone Cleaning

Supplies and Equipment:

MarbleLife, Inc.
805 W. North Carrier Pkwy, Suite 220,
Grand Prarie, TX 75050
800-627-4569, Fax 972-623-0220
www.marblelife.com

Vic International Corp.
P.O. Box 12610
Knoxville, TN 37912
800-423-1634

Training and Information:

National Training Center for
Stone and Masonry Trades
941 Longdale Avenue
Longwood, Florida 32750
407-834-4800
www.webcreations.com/marble

Swimming Pool Service

Supplies:

Most supplies and equipment can be
purchased locally.

Franchise:

PFS Swimming Pool Services
800-399-4070
www.pfspool.com

Temporary Help Service

Franchises:

Express Services, Inc.
800-652-6400
www.expresspersonnel.com

Remedy Temp, Inc.
800-828-3726
www.remedystaff.com

Trash Removal

Equipment:

Heil South
500 Lee Industrial Blvd.
Austell, Ga. 30168
800-648-1101
www.heil.com

Tree Trimming

Supplies:

Most supplies and equipment can be purchased locally.

Uniforms:

G & K Services
5995 Opus Pkwy, #500
Minnetonka, MN 55343
800-GK-CARES, Fax 612-912-5975
www.teamwear.com

WearGuard
141 Longwater Dr.
Norwell, MA 02061
781-871-4100, Fax 781-871-6239
www.wearguard.com

Water Damage Restoration

Supplies and Equipment:

Basic Maintenance Supply
2719 Edgemont St.
Philadelphia, PA 19134
800-784-8870, Fax 215-634-8878
www.cleaning-equipment.com

Freezedry Specialties, Inc.
8629 Jefferson Hwy.
Osseo, MN 55369
800-362-8380, Fax 612-425-8882
www.water-removal.com

Howe-Baker Engineers, Inc.
[ozone generators]
P.O. Box 956
Tyler, TX 75710-0956
800-323-2115, Fax 603-581-6178
e-mail: senozaire@howebaker.com

InjectDry Systems, Inc.
P.O. Box 9644, Redmond, WA 98052
800-257-0797, Fax 425-861-1812
www.injectdry.com

Training:

Jon-Don
400 Medinah Rd., Roselle, IL 60172
800-556-6366, Fax 630-893-6868
www.jondon.com

Window Cleaning

Squeegees and Equipment:

Most supplies can be purchased locally.

Clean Source
1711 Rogers Ave., San Jose, CA 95112
800-436-1907, Fax 408-436-4832

Pro-Link, Inc.
510 Chapman St., Canton, MA 02021
800-74LINKS
www.prolinkhq.com

Tucker Mfg. Co., Inc.
613 2nd Ave. SE
Cedar Rapids, IA 52401
800-553-8131, Fax 319-366-7792
www.tuckerusa.com

Awning Cleaning Supplies:

Awning Profit Systems
916 Winona Blvd., Rochester, NY 14617
Fax 716-342-3432
www.awningclean.com

Awning Rejuvanation Systems Intl.
6732 N.W. 20th Ave.
Ft. Lauderdale, FL 33309
Fax 954-971-0193
www.awningcleaning.com

Additional Reading:

Taking the Pane Out of Window Cleaning — John Baxter
Published by Crystal Press, Inc.

High Rise Window Cleaning Techniques and Equipment — C.S. Caulkins

Published by Cleaning Consultant Services, Inc.

How to Start a Window Cleaning Business — Judy Suval
Published by Cleaning Consultant Services, Inc.

Training Videos:

"Advanced Window Cleaning Techniques"
"Window Cleaning Secrets of the Professionals"
"Window Cleaning Video and Manual"
        — J. Racenstein & Co., Inc.
800-221-3748

"Window Cleaning Techniques" —
Unger Enterprises 203-366-4884, Fax 203-367-1977

Yacht Cleaning

Supplies and Equipment:

Most supplies can be purchased locally.

E & B Discount Marine
201 Meadow Road
Edison, NJ 08818
800-533-5007 or 800-262-8464
Fax 908-819-4771

Service Business Computer Programs

Rimrock Technologies
1919 Montana Ave.
Billings, Montana 59101-2842
Fax 406-248-3533
www.rimrocktech.com

Quick Books
6060 Nancy Ridge Dr., Suite 100
San Diego, CA 92121-3290
800-926-5685

Quetzal InfoSystems
1708 East 4th St.
Brooklyn, NY 11223-1925
Fax 718-645-1496
www.quetz.com

Custom Forms, Checks, Doorknob Hangers, etc.

NEBS, Inc.
500 Main St.
Groton, MA 01471
800-367-6327 ext. 50052
Fax 800-234-4324
www.nebs.com

Squid Marketing
1709 Broadway Blvd.
Toms River, NJ 08757
Fax 732-671-7378
www.querkink.com/squid/index.html

Sources of Helpful Information for Business Start-Up

Small Business Tax Information Line:
800-829-1040

Small Business Administration (SBA):
800-UASKSBA
www.sba.gov